DO YO
OWN
PR

DO YOUR OWN PR

The A-Z of Growing Your Business Through
The Press, Networking & Social Media

Paula Gardner

First Published In Great Britain 2009
by www.leanmarketingpress.com

© Copyright Paula Gardner

Typeset in Trebuchet

For Gerry

Acknowledgements

I'd like to thank Susan Moore, Kelly Molson, Dinah Gardner, Karen Thorne, Audrey Boss, Heather Waring, Alan Stevens, Nikki Pilkington, Hulya Erdal, Fiona Robyn, Nicola Cairncross, Beverley Knowles, Suzy Greaves, Hela Wozniak-Kay, Chris Toynbee, Colin Jervis, and, of course, Debbie Jenkins and Joe Gregory for all their help.

Contents

Acknowledgements
Contents

Foreword 1
Introduction 3
A 5
    Awards 5
    Articles 8
    Audrey Boss 11
B 15
    Blogging 15
    Books 17
    Beverley Knowles 19
C 23
    Collaboration 23
    Cold Calling 24
D 29
    Daily Pr Activities 29
    Differentiation 31
E 33
    Etiquette 33
    Evaluation 35
F 37
    Freelancers 37
    Facebook 39
G 41
    Google Alerts 41

GOALS 41
GROWING YOUR BUSINESS 43
H.. 49
HOOKS... 49
HEATHER WARING... 50
I... 53
INSPIRATION 53
ILLUMINATION 54
J... 59
JULIE WOODARD 59
JUNK MAIL 60
K 65
KEEPING TRACK 65
KAREN THORNE 68
L.. 73
LEARNING TO READ... 73
LOCAL PRESS 74
M 77
MEDIA REQUESTS 77
N 81
NETWORKING 81
O... 93
ONLINE PR 93
OPEN EVENTS 97
P.. 99
PR BUDDIES... 99
PRESS RELEASES 101
PERSISTENCE 105
PODCASTING.. 106
Q... 111
QUICK, QUICK, QUICK 111

R 113
   RESOURCES 113
   READING HABITS.. 114
   ROBYN WEST.. 115
   RADIO TIPS.. 118
S... 123
   SABOTAGE.. 123
   SHARYN WORTMAN...................................... 127
T... 131
   TIP SHEETS 131
   TWITTER 132
U 137
   USING A PR COMPANY 137
V 143
   VIRTUAL ASSISTANTS...................................... 143
   VACATIONS.. 144
W 145
   WHEN PR DOESN'T WORK 145
   WIN, WIN, WIN 147
X 149
   EXCITEMENT 149
Y 151
   YOU 151
   YOU TUBE.. 152
Z 155
   ZEST.. 155
Extras 157
   PRESS RELEASES.. 157
   TIP SHEETS 161
Glossary... 165
About Paula Gardner 167

What People Are Saying...

"*Brilliant, simple, hitting-the-nail-on-the-head advice makes this book an invaluable tool for businesses of any size. Large company or small, big PR budget or no budget at all, DO YOUR OWN PR tells you everything you need to know – in plain English – about raising your profile. It contains well-observed general truisms, smart technical advice and loads of specific PR-related nuggets anyone can use to boost the success of their business. The excellent Paula Gardner is doing herself and the rest of the PR industry out of a job.*"

Jamie Oliver, Business Writer, The Telegraph, Financial Times

"*I've just read your new book and I wanted to let you know that I found it really informative and highly motivational. I realised last year that there must be more to raising your profile than paid advertising and I was delighted to have the opportunity to read it to help cement my limited knowledge of traditional PR. In addition, it has provided lots of ideas and inspiration for ways in which I can incorporate social networking into my PR Plan. A year a go I would not have thought twice about such an opportunity! I would urge any small business owner looking to Do their Own PR that this is a 'must read' to provide an all round understanding of the subject. The testimonials from real business owners certainly help to pick you up when the going gets tough!*"

Amanda O'Toole, Carbis Bay Holidays

"Do Your Own PR is packed full of practical, step-by-step activities for anyone wanting to grow their business. The A-Z format is easy to follow, and the advice is always sensible and straightforward. The testimonials and case studies give the book a personal touch, and demonstrate the PR activities in action. The book also includes up to the minute information to help you navigate the Internet and make the most of social networking. Best of all, Paula encourages us to have fun with our PR!"

Fiona Robyn, author of 'The Letters'

"Finally, a real and honest approach to PR from a true talent in the field, Paula Gardner. Her no-nonsense, direct approach is mixed brilliantly with encouragement and inspiration from people who've taken Paula's advice and won! This is un-put-downable for any business trying to understand and keep up with PR in 21st century, just fabulous!"

Lynette Allen, author of 'Behind with the Mortgage and Living off Plastic'

"The problem nowadays is that small business owners don't know where to start with marketing activities. There will always be too much information and too little time. Read Paula's book and you'll take away that sense of overwhelm and learn some superb tactics that really work. I know - I've tried and tested many of them! Paula has a gift for demystifying PR and making it easy-peasy for anyone, even if the only thing you know about PR is how to spell it! This book is brilliant. If you only have a tiny budget, I can't think of a better way to invest it than this Do Your Own PR Book."

Amanda Alexander, Corporate Mothers

"So you've decided to set up on your own- congratulations. You may be passionate about what you do, but the rest of the world has never heard of you - an unfortunate reality for many new businesses. This is where Paula's great book comes in. PR is essential to your growth and livelihood but with so many media avenues available, it's often difficult to know where to start. Paula's A-Z format has simplified how, why and when you can get the most effective results for your business and how you can enjoy the journey at the same time. Her book describes the tools, explains the processes and even gives you the worst-case scenarios, so that the 'fear' factor disappears and you can choose the course of action that is right for you. Backed up with positive case studies, this book inspires not only the new business owner but also some of us who've been around a little longer! This is a book that I'll be constantly referring to for fresh ideas and an expert's 'know-how'. If you're a business owner, committed to success, I suggest you should too."

Sue Donnelly, Feelfabat50.com

Foreword

Doing Your Own PR requires bravery because you are about to put your head above the parapet and be seen. And it can be terrifying. What if we make a fool of ourselves, what if we fail, what if we're not good enough, what if everyone laughs, points and sneers?

I always say my Big Leaping coaching clients succeed not that we are so much talented or special than the rest, we're just braver. We dare to put our heads above the parapet and dare to fail, to succeed, to be seen, to go for it.

I'm forever inspired by the bestselling author Marianne Williamson, who says in her book Return to Love: "Our deepest fear is not that we inadequate. Our deepest fear is that we are powerful beyond measure. It is our light, not our darkness that frightens us. We ask ourselves, Who am I to be brilliant, gorgeous, talented, fabulous? Actually, who are you not to be?"

Paula has written a wonderfully inspiring and practical book on the nuts and bolts on how to get out there and do your own PR. But the first question, I want to ask is you is - do you dare?

But don't panic if right this second, you don't. It is a process. What I'm learning is that when you write a book, or write an article, or your blog or press release, you get to put your thoughts in order and start to birth and hone your philosophy and what you really believe, which in turn starts to boost your confidence in yourself and what you have to offer.

The first step can often be the hardest. When I wrote my first book Making The Big Leap, I thought I would be exposed as a big fat fake. Who was I to write a book? What did I know? I didn't even realise I had a philosophy but by writing it down, by talking to my clients, I realised that I did. I wasn't some fake, I actually knew what I was talking about and that this process worked! My book then became a brilliant vehicle for spreading my message about what I really believed in.

PR often gets a bad name. We feel embarrassed that we're 'selling' ourselves or blowing our own trumpet. But what if you could see PR not as some horrible grubby hard sell but just simply a way to beam your messages out into the world? For most of us when we start our own businesses, we couldn't and wouldn't do it if we weren't passionate about what we do or didn't believe in it. Yes, it is about selling units/seats/stuff too but PR is primarily a brilliant opportunity to communicate your message and that passion to the world.

So be brave, take your first step and use this fantastically practical and inspirational book to launch your PR campaigns so you can sing your message to bigger and bigger audiences. Guaranteed it's scary at first but I would encourage you to be simply 'brilliant, gorgeous, talented and fabulous'. Go on, you know you want to.

Suzy Greaves
Founder of The Big Leap Coaching Company
www.thebig-leap.com

Introduction

When I wrote my first book, *Get Noticed*, I had no idea how much difference it would make to my business, and how many people it would bring into my life. It's brought me friends, hundreds of new clients, and has been a vital tool in establishing my company *Do Your Own PR* as one of the top choices for small businesses who want to learn how to do their own PR.

But *Get Noticed* came out five years ago and, whilst all the exercises within those pages will work equally well today, things have moved on. The lines between PR and marketing have blurred. The Internet plays a much larger part in any campaign than it did before, and the options available on the Internet, from social networking sites such as Facebook to article placing on syndication sites, have grown phenomenally.

Indeed, if you are a one-man business, or small business with limited resources (including time) then you will find the amount of choice overwhelming. There is almost too much that you could do. Five years ago my one to one consultations often consisted of showing people how to use a limited range of options to help them grow their business. Today, much of my consultation time goes on working out which selection of tools, from the huge range available, will work for them and their business.

And that's what I've set out to do with this book, *Do Your Own PR*. Presented in an A-Z format, it allows you to browse the different PR activities available to you, and pick and choose which ones should work for you. I've tried to bring it as up to date as I can by including the online options that I know have worked for many of my clients. But of course, even as this book goes to print, new and previously unheard of sites and tools will be springing up.

Something else I have decided to do is to pepper the book with first person accounts from my clients. These are ordinary people who have adopted some of my advice and achieved significant success with their PR activities. From them you'll hear the good, the bad and the ugly. You'll hear what's really worked for them, and what just didn't justify the time they spent on it. My sincere thanks goes to them for allowing me to use their stories, which will, I hope, inspire you to get going and take some action.

And that's what it's all about. Taking action. Doing something. By all means read this book through, but never forget that A also stands for action.

Have fun!

Paula Gardner

A

AWARDS

Entering and winning business awards (or even reaching a finalist position), is a great method of boosting press coverage and many awarding bodies, such as the big banks, also do a great job of publicising their winners.

The big thing that puts people off entering these awards is the work that goes into it, but it's important to remember that once you've done the work a lot of it can be tweaked and tailored for your next entry. They will all need a different approach. One might focus on creativity, another on staff training for instance, but much of the content will be the same. So, here are my top eleven suggestions to give you the best chance of getting noticed by the judges.

1. MAKE THE DECISION TO DO IT

If you are bringing entering awards into your PR programme then really do go for it. Just half-heartedly entering one award is a waste of your time. Do your research and see how many you are actually eligible for. In my case I found over ten in a 30-second web search.

Likewise, give yourself the resources you need to do the job. Bring in outside help, such as copywriting if you need it, as this is a big investment in your future.

2. THERE'S NO PLACE FOR MODESTY

Whilst you don't want to sound too smug or to gloat, you do need to get your head around being proud of what you've achieved, and how you've done it.

3. DO SOME DIGGING

Who won last year and the year before that? Find out why and maybe even speak to them if you can. Can they tell you what they think was the deciding factor in their favour?

4. PUNCH AT THE RIGHT WEIGHT

One of my clients entered the company category of an award, rather than the freelance section. She did it because she wanted to look bigger than she was, and she did ok, even got a special mention. But when one of the judges accidentally revealed that had she entered the freelance section she would have won hands down she was gutted.

5. READ THE RULES AND USE THE SPACE!

If you don't cover everything they are looking for then your entry is likely to fail to make the grade. And when it comes to filling the page, I keep telling my secondary-school age son that the fact they've given you a whole page on a comprehension exercise means that they feel that there is enough information there to merit a page. Likewise with an award, one-line answers are not enough. Equally, be just as careful not to go over the word limit.

6. TREAT IT AS PITCH

Give your entry structure, with headings and bullet points to make it easy on the eye. Logos and graphics make it look stylish and neat.

7. GIVE IT SOME PERSONALITY

I think that adding that little story about the reason you came to start the company, or the little anecdote behind the business name gives an entry colour and sometimes even humour. This is bound to make it all the more attractive and memorable. Likewise, pay special attention to your opening and beginning paragraphs as these hold a lot of sway.

8. MAKE SURE IT'S NEAT

I'm sure I don't need to say it but I will anyway; make sure it's neat! Also, get someone (not on your team) to proof read it before it goes in. It may make sense to you but what about to someone who knows nothing about your business?

9. START PLANNING FOR FUTURE AWARDS

Keep a diary or craft your blog entries, and include little snippets of info and news about your business that you'll be able to lift for future awards.

10. DON'T GIVE UP

Think of this as an ongoing activity and keep at it.

11. IF YOU WIN, MAKE THE MOST OF IT!

Go to the award ceremony (do this even if you don't win) and get that press release out there as soon as possible. Liaise with the awarding body's PR department to see how you can help them do their job and whizz off an email to your existing clients and mailing list and tell them your great news.

I'll leave you with this quote from my fabulous VA, Susan Moore of *www.mooreva.co.uk* who won Outstanding VA of the Year Award in 2008.

"Winning Outstanding VA of the Year Award has benefited my business in many ways. I had several potential clients who were considering using a VA and in the week after my win they decided to sign up - no coincidence, I'm sure. The Award also brought me into contact with other high calibre VAs and business owners with whom I could set up alliances, which enabled me to build a strong team. I also think that when I've contacted journalists offering to write on the subject, it has definitely helped to open doors. Lastly, and by no means least, some of my favourite clients like to tell other businesses that their VA has won a national award - there's no downside!"

ARTICLES

Many of my clients are experts at what they do and understand that one of the best ways to PR yourself and your business is to write articles. Writing articles about your area of expertise helps you build credibility, forge good relationships with the press and can sound much less "pushy" than putting out a press release.

However, I'm not just talking about writing articles and putting them out on article syndication sites - although this is a must for anyone who wants good PR and SEO[1] in one fell swoop – but also sending them to off the shelf traditional publications and independent websites.

But there are rules when it comes to approaching publications, ones that will make your life easier, and give your articles the best chance of reaching the newstands.

1. FOCUS

Think about which publications you'll be targeting. Many of the people who sign up for my writing article ecourse say they want to write for Pyschologies magazine, GQ or The Sunday Times. To be frank, unless they're already high profile or have a background in journalism, that is unlikely to happen. You are better off striking at smaller publications and building up to the higher circulation ones as you progress.

2. RESEARCH

Check who makes the decisions on editorial and commissioning. Look at the masthead for names like Features Ed or Commissioning Editor.

---

[1] Search Engine Optimisation - The better your site is optimised, the more likely it is to be found in the first few pages of a web search. One way to optimise your site is to have as many links as possible from good quality websites.

3. TALK IT THROUGH

Never send out a completed article - talk the idea through first or send a synopsis. It's more than likely that, if they like your idea, they'll want to add their own slant or angle and the brief will be slightly different to the one you approached them with.

4. ONE BY ONE

Unlike press releases which can go out en masse, only approach one publication at a time and move onto the next one when you've got their answer. Let them know you're doing this though, and give them a deadline so you're not left hanging around waiting for their reply.

5. SHOW YOUR STUFF

Build up a portfolio of work, even if it's just links to articles on the Internet, that you can show them.

6. GET HELP

Can't write but you still have lots of ideas and knowledge that you know would make good reading? Use a ghost-writer and get them to craft your articles for you. Any good copywriter should be able to offer this service.

7. CRAFT

Take the time to make your synopsis the best it can be - this is the thing that will sell your article for you.

8. GIVE THEM WHAT THEY WANT

Think about what the publication will want. For example, do they tend to feature celebrities a lot? If so, alluding to them in your piece is more likely to sit well with that title. Are they a serious journal that includes facts, figures and in depth references to sources? If so, make sure that you've got everything you need to stand up to scrutiny.

9. MAKE SURE THEY WANT YOU

Make sure there's a good reason for you to write the piece (i.e. your research or contacts) that stops the editor from nabbing your idea and giving it to a staff member to write up - believe me, it does happen.

10. BE PROFESSIONAL

If you do get commissioned make sure you ask about deadlines, number of words etc and deliver well on time. This is the time to build up a reputation as a reliable professional.

AUDREY BOSS

Audrey is the first of a small number of case studies that you'll find throughout this book. I've used clients who have worked with me personally and who have gone onto doing their own PR extremely well. I think it's important that you hear about the realities of PR not just from me, but ordinary business owners who have just rolled up their sleeves and got on with it.

Audrey Boss of *www.beyondchocolate.co.uk* has, over the years, blossomed and moved dramatically forwards PR-wise. I believe that she is a really inspiring case study for us all!

"I'd like to say that I have a regular slot dedicated to PR but the reality is quite different. Running a small business means I am often reacting to emergencies rather than being proactive! Having said that I work on PR in three ways: I have a monthly PR coaching session with an excellent Do Your Own PR coach which really helps me to focus on the PR objectives I want to reach and gets me thinking on how I want to reach them. It also means I'm accountable to someone from one month to another so it spurs me to get things done! I'd say this generates anywhere between 1 to 2 days' work a month.

"Another way I work on PR is by regularly reading magazines and papers I'm interested in being featured in and cutting out articles I come across by journalists I think could be 'sympathetic' to Beyond Chocolate. I can't say exactly how much time I spend doing this, as it's an ongoing activity. Lastly I respond to PR 'urgencies' when I have an event coming up or think I can use a big story in the press as a hook. In these moments I can spend up to 3 or 4 days working solely on PR - writing the press release, making press packs, sending it all out and following up with calls.

"I'm very lucky in that I run workshops on a subject which appeals to most women and journalists love a freebie which means that I can 'showcase' my work quite effortlessly. I reserve at least one space on each workshop I run for journalists. Sometimes I actively invite someone from a magazine or newspaper I'm interested in but more often they get in touch with me and ask for a free place in exchange for a feature of some kind. This has produced some of our best PR such as being featured in the June

2007 'Tried & Tested' column of Psychologies and other features in titles such as *www.handbag.com* and Glamour magazine. I've also found it works to keep all my PR contacts informed of any news, especially if I can suggest a feature idea they can pitch to their editor or to a magazine if they are freelance.

"I've learned that journalists really like it when you do as much of the work as possible for them and provide them with the 'full package'. This usually includes an interesting statistic, fact or case study, an idea for a feature, a few pictures and, if possible, a link to a current affairs subject or to a celebrity (distasteful as this is!)

"I have a good relationship with several freelancers with whom I keep in touch on a regular basis. I am also developing relationships with editors on several key magazines.

"I'm not keen on calling to find out who I need to speak to and send press releases to. People are busy and usually don't have much time for cold callers so it's never very pleasant and *always* very time consuming. I'm getting to grips with modern tools of PR. I have been giving Podcasting more and more thought. We know what content we would have but it's finding time to do more that's proving difficult.

"The only one we've started actually using is Facebook. We are supposed to be using it to get the word out but we don't really get round to it. On the other hand, we have tested a small ad campaign which has yielded surprisingly good results.

"We've had several high points over the past few months. I think being called personally by the editor of Psychologies because she wanted to know more about Beyond

Chocolate and hearing how enthusiastic she is was great (as well as being featured in Psychologies three months in a row!) Also, getting a full-page feature in Metro after cold calling the health editor - that was fantastic!

"I've learnt that you have to persevere. Don't give up. Just because someone doesn't have the time to speak to you or is short on the phone and doesn't sound interested it doesn't mean they're not and won't end up featuring you. Keep on at them, as long they're not saying NO, anything is possible. All publicity is good publicity. I used to get really upset at the beginning when features trivialised what we did or misquoted us or seemed to present Beyond Chocolate in a negative light but ANY mention in the press brings contacts!

"You also need to do as much groundwork as possible for the journalist or editor. Don't just send a standard press release. Send an interesting story, a hook, some facts and figures, pictures and links to resources. Don't give up. Prep work massively improves your chances. If you really don't like cold calling, get an assistant or a friend to help you. Make a list of all the media you are interested in getting into and then call to find out exactly what you need to send to whom, when and in what format.

"If you've got something free to give away - use it!

"Every time we get mentioned in the media, whether it's a tiny quote in a magazine or an interview on a late night radio programme or a full blown feature in a newspaper, we see a massive boost in newsletter subscribers over the next few days and a consequent rise in bookings. It's magic!"

B

BLOGGING

Blog, short for web log, is basically nothing more than an online diary. People use it to record thoughts and events (which can range from political opinions to what they had for breakfast that day). But what we are interested in is using it as a promotional tool.

Blogging, in my opinion, is best for businesses that revolve around a person, a figurehead, who stands for the brand of the company. That way people can get to know you and your approach.

You can go for the commentary approach, giving your opinion on what's happening out there, or in your industry. Or, you can adopt the more personal tone, and help people get to know the person behind the business. Many Internet marketeers use blogs as a way to bombard people with advice, attracting people through the amount of free advice and information that they give away.

Blogging has another advantage. From an SEO (search engine optimisation) point, a blog is normally updated much more regularly than a website and so more likely to get higher rankings within the search engines. So you can think of a blog as a teaser, to get people to visit and then, hopefully, click through to your website.

You can set up a free blog at *www.blogger.com* or, for a slightly more intuitive set-up www.typepad.com charges a small monthly fee. These will normally be hosted at a different address to your website, although the top package on Typepad allows you to direct the blog to your business address so that the address looks like a normal website address.

Alternatively, get your own web people to set one up for you and host it on your own site.

Blogs also have a facility called an RSS feed (really simple syndication) which means that people who are interested in your blog can have updates sent direct to their inbox as and when you upload them.

Blogging only works if you do it regularly, and that's the big challenge. Half hearted blogs soon lose their fans and I know this from personal experience! If I'm busy blogging is the first thing that slips.

Just like magazines and websites, you can target other people's blogs as part of your PR campaign. One way to do this is to leave comments on other people's postings, including your signature to lead people to your website. Another way to do this, especially relevant if you have a product to publicise, is to offer bloggers your product to review, something that is commonplace now within the IT industry.

Finally, here's a quote from someone who whom blogging worked remarkably well.

"Paula has plenty of good ideas and converts consultations into action plans, which she then follows up. In particular, Paula inspired me to start a blog and after 7 months the blog gets about 1000 visits a day and has attracted interest in my sector and with the media."
Colin Jervis, Managing Director,
www.kineticconsulting.co.uk

BOOKS
THE SECRETS OF WRITING A NON-FICTION BOOK

People often ask me about my first book, *Get Noticed*. How long did it take to write? How did I find the time? What impact has it had on my business? And I always say that nothing beats writing a non-fiction book as a way to boost your credibility, income and publicity.

DECIDING WHAT TO WRITE

Almost all of the clients I see have an idea for a book in there somewhere, often bubbling just beneath the surface. But, similarly, sometimes when they describe their great idea I've got a funny niggly feeling that I've heard it before… and I probably have. So the first thing that you should do is check out the competition. What other titles are there on your chosen subject and how do they compare to the book you want to write? And how can you make yours better?

If there aren't any then it's could be time to start rubbing your hands with glee… or give up on the idea altogether as it may mean there's little or no market. Investigate further!

CHEAT A LITTLE

I must admit that I was very lucky when it came to writing my first book *Get Noticed* as I had about a year's worth of newsletters that I could use to give structure and content to the book. What I had to do was turn my material into a realistic and practical course that worked, as well as made sense. The good news is that if you've been writing newsletters for a while you probably have got a lot of ready-made material for your book already. Now, does that seem less scary?

YOU DON'T HAVE TO DO THE WHOLE THING AT ONCE

Publishers often don't want to wade through the whole book initially so if you've got a couple of chapters and a synopsis already then you can get things moving and get those out to publishers and carry on with the rest of the writing whilst you wait.

GET INSPIRED

If you find it hard to get in the flow try a few weeks of the morning pages exercise as shown in Julia Cameron's fantastic book *The Artist's Way*.

PUT IT INTO EBOOK FORMAT

This means that you can test the market, gauge reactions and change the book a little if necessary. You can also sell the book from your own website and keep all the profits.

BLOG IT!

Disciplining yourself to write a blog regularly means that you'll not only be boosting your business, helping search engine optimisation but also helping build up material for your book - and this works with fiction just as much as non-fiction.

BEVERLEY KNOWLES

Beverley runs a contemporary art gallery in Ladbroke Grove (*www.beverleyknowles.com*) that specialises in women artists.

"The best thing I've done PR-wise has probably been the writing, which Paula suggested I start doing in the first place. I get quite a lot of feedback from the newsletters we email out and it seems to get passed around from one person to another. The more I've written the more pleasure I've got out of it too and it's become a way of getting featured in publications in itself, which of course is good for PR.

"Getting in with local glossies has also been helpful. We're lucky in Ladbroke Grove because there are a few and they always seem interested to hear what we're up to and are happy to be supportive of local initiatives.

"I find it difficult to know sometimes what is working and what isn't. Who was it who said that only 5% of their marketing produced any results only they didn't know which 5%? It feels like that a lot of the time.

"Sometimes it's just a matter of luck. Somebody I knew happened to know Antony Gormley from art college days. My friend's wife had some work in an exhibition here so Antony Gormley came to show support for his friend, so the private view snaps had Antony Gormley, so the local magazine featured them in the party section. Quite a few people came down to the gallery after purely on the basis of that and we made quite a bit of business as a direct result. But I couldn't have planned that. We just got lucky. On the other hand it's useful to be aware that personal or personality endorsement is a big thing, particularly when you're selling expensive and sometimes enigmatic things like art.

"Only 2% of my business last year came from passing trade. It's all word of mouth and endorsement, and PR is a part of that.

"I'm on good terms with the editors and arts page writers of all the local glossies and a few journalists from the broadsheets. I need to step it up a gear now and start calling up the scarier journalists, the more academic art writers from the weightier publications. Endorsement from them means a lot in the art business.

"It's this ringing that I enjoy the least, not so much because I'm nervous of speaking to the press because I'm not really any more. I've finally figured out that they're just people like you and me. More because it's such a waste of time in terms of the amount of time spent not getting through to the person you need to speak to. Either they've moved jobs or they're 'away from their desk' (what a ridiculous phrase that is, as if usually they're chained to it).

"Results in PR are difficult to measure so I'd say what I enjoy most is seeing my own written work in print and especially getting feed back about it.

"The goalposts are constantly changing though. The first time we got into The Times I thought I was going to burst with excitement. Now when we get into The Times I'm like great and what else has been going on?

"PR doesn't necessarily translate directly into sales. PR is very useful but selling still has to be pursued in its own right.

Journalists are human (most of them!) Try to make your press releases personally engaging; anecdotes and quirky things grab people's attention far more effectively than reams of geeky product information. Remember that it's a person who is reading it, not a computer and that person receives hundreds of releases every day. The best way to get noticed is to reach out to them in a personal way."

Paula Gardner

C

COLLABORATION

Collaboration has been a big, big factor in building my business, especially in the early days. It's fun, stimulating and you can always learn stuff by working with other people, even if it is only for a short time.

I've built my mailing list by offering other Internet marketers material for their newsletters or websites, or even special offers for their clients and mailing list. I gave new members of one high profile women's networking company a free 30 minute coaching session when they joined the networking group – and consequently landed myself new clients who hadn't until then even heard of me.

The most pleasurable collaborations I have done have been offline. I arranged low-key evening networking events with both Dawn Winder of I-Define and Kelly Molson of Rubbercheese. We found a bar in Soho that was happy to give us a free room on a Monday evening, invited along all the people that we were regularly in touch with, people that we wanted to get to know, and just chatted to them on the night. It was a great way to grow our lists in a very enjoyable low stress manner.

Other collaborations you might like to consider are getting together with other business owners to offer a fantastic competition prize – you own a hotel, your friend owns a hair salon and you know of a life coach. It's a short step to meeting for coffee and deciding to collaborate and offer a local newspaper the chance for one lucky reader to have a make over day. This could be a day with a life coach, with a free hair cut and pampering stay at your hotel to top it all off. What would have been difficult to get into the local newspaper on its own now becomes much more attractive, and there's no reason why you can't go on to repeat this with different publications and even local radio, over and over again.

COLD CALLING

It's a rare person that doesn't hate cold calling, and to be frank, you probably will always feel uncomfortable about doing it. It is human nature to prefer not to set ourselves up for rejection, and cold calling is doing just that - allowing someone else to reject us.

Let me tell you about a boy that I knew at University. His name was Sean and he was a friend of one of my best friends. I didn't like him. I thought he was a smarmy git who pestered every woman within 5 feet of him (without discrimination) until they either gave in and went out on a date with him, or told him in no uncertain terms where to go. Needless to say I was one of the latter.

Now, believe it or not but Sean was a hero for many of my male friends. Yes, they could see that he was an irritating sexist predator but, while they sat around mooning over pictures of Madonna he was actually out there and getting dates, because, yes, you guessed it, out of some of the women that he tried a percentage actually said yes.

Sean played the numbers game. He knew that the more women he asked out the more likely he was to get dates. And, although he knew that he would get rejected, over and over again, the dates, when they came, were worth the set-backs. Sean had the best sex life on campus.

Now, I would consider that this method of asking and asking until you get is like cold calling at its most unsophisticated. But, Sean can teach us a vital lesson, and that is: Doing your best and then distancing yourself from the verdict helps protect you. Without that ability to let go and move onto your next target, you'll flounder.

So, how do you do this? First, think about what the worst-case scenario would be. If it's a journalist you are calling the chances are that:

- They might be busy and you are calling at a busy time.

- You are trying to sell a story that is just not of interest to them.

- You've spoken to them recently and have nothing new to add and therefore might come over as a bit of a pest.

- You just clam up and sound silly.

So, what can you do about it?

- Ask if this is a good time to call to quickly run something past them, with the emphasis on the quickly. If it isn't say you will call back and ask when the best time would be. And then do it.
- Do your homework and make sure that you present it in a way that ties in with their publication's stories and readership.
- Always make sure that you have something to offer when calling (samples, news story etc) and don't call 'just to check if you got the press release'.
- Be prepared with a script (we go into that later) and try to relax before-hand.

And, if the worst happens, remember that editorial offices are busy places and, believe me, they will have forgotten about your call long before you do.

GETTING THROUGH TO THE RIGHT PERSON

The trick to getting through to the right person is to not even try on your first go. Your initial call should merely be seen as a fact gathering exercise to find out who is the best person to talk to about this, or the best person to send a press release to. When it comes to publications you might get this sort of information off a receptionist, but you'll probably need to speak to someone in editorial.

Ask if the person in question prefers to be contacted through email or post, and what time of the day or week is the best to get in touch with them. You can ask for their direct line at the same time if you're feeling brave. A sample script might be:

> Switchboard: "Hello, wonderful magazines."
>
> Me: "Hello, can I speak to someone on editorial at Well Written magazine please?"
>
> Editorial at Well Written magazine: "Hello, editorial."
>
> Me: "Hi there, I'm sending in some information on a company that does blah blah and wondered who would be the best person to send it to?"
>
> Them: "That would be Matt Hack."
>
> Me: "Great, thanks. Could you give me his email address please? ..."

If you have to ascertain a number of people (fashion editor, IT editor, careers editor) on the same magazine you might well have to call and do the same process over and over again. The person on the other end might not be too pleased about being a telephone directory for the next ten minutes.

This is why I suggest leaving your real selling talk to another time, when you are not so focused on a fact-finding mission. Even if the person on the end of the line says, "That's me," don't be tempted to launch into your spiel. Save it for another time when you are more psyched up for it.

KNOWING WHAT TO SAY

Nothing beats having a script. It helps keep you focused and provides you with a prompt if you forget what you were going to say. When you've written it down and read it back to yourself (or a colleague or willing partner) then you should have a better idea if it really cuts the ice.

As you become more confident or just interact with the human being on the other side, you will find yourself veering off from the script. But, even now, I always write out a script before I embark on a cold calling session.

Finally, getting in the right mood is vital. Take your time and rev up for it – playing some high-energy music if you like, or phoning a few customers to get in the mood for sales talk.

D

DAILY PR ACTIVITIES

READ

Read a different publication every day. This could be a daily paper, a trade publication, women's magazine, a men's mag, hobby or travel magazine. Pick up something you normally wouldn't touch. It will provide you with ideas and hooks that you can hang your press release on to make it topical. It will also keep you in touch with who is hot and who isn't. That could mean anything from celebrities to people in high finance, depending on your area of interest.

My suggestion is to build this into your daily work routine; taking yourself off somewhere quiet and reading through the publication for content. Next you should scan it for ideas and themes that you can use in your press release. For instance, if you are a plastic surgeon and the latest gossip is that a certain Hollywood name has had something done, this can be a great hook for your next press release.

LEARN

Your next task is to look at how other businesses have got themselves into the publication – is it through reviews, surveys, great photos? What can you learn from them? Also, make sure that you vary your publications as this will keep things fresh and give you a good overview.

EXPAND

Your third daily task is to add a journalist or publication to your media list. This could be from the publication that you've read, or just the contact details for a website that you've come across on the net. Compiling your media list as you go makes the whole thing seem much less daunting.

CONNECT

The next thing I think you should be doing is connecting with three people every day. These could be people that you've met at networking events, exhibitions or conferences, past or current clients or journalists. Think of this as an energy thing as much as straight PR – the more effort you make in putting yourself out there and reminding people that you are there, the more you get back. It might take a while and it might not boomerang back from the people that you made contact with in the first place, but it will happen.

DIFFERENTIATION

Last year I gave a talk to The Federation of Wedding Planners. It was an unusual occasion, as everyone in the room did the same thing and could, potentially, be the next person's competition. Hmm, tricky. So, as part of the proceedings I asked everyone to talk about their USP (unique selling point), why they are different.

It was a fascinating exercise, as it soon became obvious that everyone was unique. Sometimes these differences were geographical, sometimes they were due to target market, or that target market's budget, and now and again they were just down to personality.

But it emphasised how important it is that you stand out from all the rest, both to potential clients and customers, and also to press.

But, how exactly do you do that? Here are some suggestions.

LOOK AT YOUR COMPETITION.

Access as much info on them as you can and start a folder on them. Look at their websites, brochures, or even mystery shop (or get a friend or colleague to do it for you) so that you can experience them first hand. One of my own clients owns a chain of Indian restaurants but still eats at one of his competitors' venues at least once a week. Of course they know him now, and they know that they are being judged, but it does help him to keep an eye on what the competition are doing and make sure that he's staying ahead.

WHAT DO YOU DO DIFFERENTLY?

What do customers remember about you, and indeed why do they choose you above your competitors in the first place? Is it strong enough to become the crux of your press campaign? Ask them.

STRENGTHEN

What can you do to make that difference stronger, or, if it's just not enough, what else can you do? Find your strengths and embrace and shout about them. There are other people offering PR training as well as myself, but many of them aim at the corporate market, whilst others do it as an aside to their day to day business. My difference is that I work with small and growing businesses and this is my main business, not something I've tacked on. When I tell this to the press they can see a difference straight away.

E

ETIQUETTE

PR Etiquette that is. Believe it or not, but there is an acceptable way to approach the press. A lot of it just boils down to old-fashioned good manners, just like any other form of communication, but it's worth just going over the basics.

If you get a journalist on the phone, it's polite to ask if now is a good time to speak. If it isn't, ask when would be a good time to call back. If you just blather on with your pitch and they've got an editor breathing down their neck over a deadline, they're never going to pay it the attention it deserves, so give yourself the best shot you can.

Again, just like making friends, you can't rush these things. As owner and editor of *www.chicklit.co.uk* I get a lot of PR people phoning me up and my pet hate is someone that launches into gush speak, asking how I am like a long lost friend. It puts me on the wrong foot, as I'm silently thinking, "Who is the person. Have I lost my mind and forgotten them?" Actually, from their point of view, I'd be better off concentrating on what they say.

It's polite to have actually read the publication that you're pitching to, but it's amazing how many people don't. It's even better if you can also comment on something that came out in a recent edition to show that you've not only read the publication but also something that they have personally written.

If a journalist leaves you a message respond to them as soon as possible. Leaving a journalist hanging only means that they will go on to the next person on their list, and mark you off as hard to reach for the future.

It's always better to send a journalist a hand-crafted personal message rather than a round-robin email sent to 200 contacts.

If you've promised a journalist something and it falls through, let them know as soon as possible so that they can find something to fill the space.

Never leave messages if you're just cold calling a journalist. First, it allows them to ignore it, but, second, once you've left two or more you start to sound like a stalker.

If you are responding to a media request it's polite to keep to topic. By all means send them stuff in future, as long as you know that what you are doing/selling is relevant to them. There's no sense in building up a completely non-targeted media list just for the sake of it.

If a journalist covers you, say thank you. You don't have to gush; just a straight-forward thanks can make all the difference.

Get their name right! Double check if you have to, and if you don't know how to pronounce it, just come out with saying something like "… that's a really unusual name, how do you pronounce it properly?"

EVALUATION

A growing percentage of my clients are businesses that have already been using a PR agency, and either finding them ineffectual or just unsure as to whether there's any real connection between the coverage they are getting and the sales they are making.

Whilst the first problem needs to be dealt with on a case to case basis, the second is something that actually needs addressing before you take on a PR agency, or even embark on your own PR campaign. It's about putting in systems to measure PR from the very beginning - or as soon as you possibly can.

There are many ways to do this and here are my top three.

1. GET ACCESS TO YOUR WEB STATS

It's amazing how many small businesses don't know how many people are clicking through to their site and from where. This is such a vital step when it comes to planning and growing an online PR campaign. Sign up for *www.statcounter.com* and you can see who is visiting your website and where they've come from in real time terms. Fantastic.

2. ASK WHERE PEOPLE HEARD ABOUT YOU

This can be in the form of a question on your contact form, or just something you naturally ask new customers. Most are quite keen to spill the beans.

3. RUN READER OFFERS

Running specific offers with specific publications will help you gauge whether it really is your target market. If someone is writing about you see if you can also add on a reader offer (most publications are usually delighted if they are already doing something on you anyway), or give a voucher number. You want to see if the people who read your PR are also taking the vital step and buying from you.

F

FREELANCERS

Getting hold of good freelance contact details is one of the biggest challenges of PR. As they don't work from the office it's almost impossible to reach them by phone, and of course, most publications will never give out their contact details. However, building a good list of freelancers on your media list is vital. So, how can you do this?

RESPOND TO MEDIA REQUESTS

You can sometimes see posts from the press in online forums or networking groups. Often they will be asking for case studies or, in some cases, experts on a particular subject. Responding to these, or just keeping the journalist's details if they are relevant, is one way to build up your freelance contacts. It can be time consuming to trawl through forums and web posts to find these, so I set up the Divine Publicity Club to do just that. I find these media requests and send them straight into your inbox and you can action them at once. Check out the *www.doyourownpr.com* website for details.

BUY A LIST

This works best with niche journalists who have their own association or group such as the Circle of Wine Writers or Guild of Travel Writers. You can purchase a list of members and get a good pre-qualified list. These can sometimes add up to a few hundred pounds so, if you know someone who would also be targeting the same list, make a joint purchase and share the cost.

LOOK AT THE PUBLICATIONS

Some publications, especially national newspapers, actually do print a freelancer's email address at the bottom of an article. Often it's a generic paula.gardner@telegraph.co.uk but it's better than nothing.

POST IT

Things sent in the post have more chance of being sent on than emails.

GOOGLE OR FACEBOOK THEM

Freelancers are business people, just like you and me, and most of them have their own websites to sell their writing wares. So, if you've seen an article by a particular writer that you want to contact try Googling them, or seeing if they've got a Facebook page.

FACEBOOK

Many people have been able to incorporate *www.facebook.com* into their PR campaigns. One of them is coach Suzy Greaves of *www.thebig-leap.com*, who runs a Big Peace club on the site. She uses Facebook as a method of collecting names and then marketing to them virally. Whenever she puts an event up everyone in her club on Facebook, and their friends, can see it.

Another way of using it is to 'make friends' with journalists, and either receive case study and media requests from them or include them in your own updates. They obviously need to agree to this, so anything you send out can't be too salesy.

But one danger with Facebook is the way it blurs personal and professional lives. For instance, it's quite possible for a friend to 'tag' you in a photo. This means that they put a photo online and a message goes out on your profile that you've been tagged, along with a link to the photo. Now anyone in your network can then go and take a look. If the photo happens to be of you masquerading as a red eyed vampire, Mrs Double Chin 2009, or, perish the thought, looking slightly the worse for wear after a night on the town with your mates, it's there for everyone to see. Nice.

Paula Gardner

G

GOOGLE ALERTS

These are a fantastic resource for anyone undertaking a PR campaign, indeed anyone in business. Google alerts are a great way of monitoring online coverage. You sign up to Google Alerts (*www.googlealerts.com*) and then an alert will automatically drop into your inbox every time someone mentions your website on the web. You can sign up for alerts on anything - even your competitors (which can be very interesting).

When you first sign up you'll find a huge amount of alerts coming through as the programme scans the net for your criteria, and some of these links may be years old. But once you're past that you should be aiming to get nice regular alerts linking to new pages as often as possible.

GOALS

I believe that it's not a good idea to set PR goals over which you have no control. So, saying that, "I'd like three national features and a competition in the next three months," whilst focusing you, can easily backfire, as you have no real control over this happening.

It's much better to set yourself goals that actually list the work you will do to get what you want. So, for instance, each month I set myself these goals alongside the coaching and PR consultations with my clients:

- Write one press and send it out to relevant press.
- Get PR Tips out to the press.
- I put out 1-2 "Get Noticed" newsletters: my newsletter for anyone who has visited the Do Your Own PR site and wants to know more about PR.
- I use the article from one of these newsletter and post it on as many sites and submit to as many newsletters etc as possible (a minimum of 30).
- Blog 2-3 times a week.
- Answer relevant media requests as they come in.

On top of that I also write a bi-monthly newsletter, Building The Buzz, for clients of Do Your Own PR.

Now, I don't manage this every month and the first thing that tends to slip is the blogging, but those are my goals. And, as I've honed the list over time I know that they are my limits too. I cannot physically do more without someone else doing it for me or abandoning my paying clients, which is obviously not on.

Since adopting this it's now become my system, a sort of mini PR factory, and it's what I teach my clients – take on as much PR as you can, then concentrate on doing that month in, month out and it will start to show results.

So, what would you have on your monthly list of goals?

GROWING YOUR BUSINESS

PR and marketing will help your business become more successful. But the obvious downside of a successful business is that you personally will no longer have as much time to devote to PR and marketing.

It's important to look at ways to deal with this eventuality so that you aren't left floundering or in a complete panic. You need to set up working systems so that you can not only cope, but are confident that you can still carry out a well-planned and effective PR campaign.

Ultimately you have three choices.

1. To grow but still retain control personally, of all your PR and marketing. It may sound great but this is very stressful and if you're planning on doing your PR and marketing full time then why aren't you running a PR company? To carry out this option successfully you'll need to be extremely disciplined. But, we do have a solution!

2. To hand over PR and marketing responsibilities to another member or members of staff.

3. To employ outside help from a PR company or practitioner.

BREAKING IT DOWN

Let's take a look at what doing your own PR long-term actually involves. Whether you are planning to outsource your PR or not this will give you a breakdown of the different tasks involved.

RESEARCH

This involves keeping up to date with newspapers, trade and professional publications, magazines, radio shows, TV shows and sometimes even blogs. This might mean getting rid of any outdated notions that sitting down and reading a newspaper when you could be doing something more productive instead is lazy. Taking time out to read and absorb what is going on around you is vital.

PLANNING YOUR PR STRATEGY

This includes market research into what image you need to project to your potential customers and devising a plan with a suitable timescale.

BUILDING RELATIONSHIPS WITH JOURNALISTS AND EDITORS

This could involve lunches, networking and going to trade events where you know they will be covering stories.

WRITING PR MATERIAL

This could include web pages, press releases, articles for inclusion on your own and other websites (in exchange for links), articles for the press, newsletters and regular tips and hints for editors.

DAY TO DAY PR

Chasing up press releases and phoning journalist with a story; giving interviews; following up past 'bites' or interviews to see when articles are being published; arranging for photos, links, photographs etc; placing competitions; buying publications and organising cuttings to most effectively impress potential clients.

And of course, co-ordinating all the above so that they run smoothly.

USING YOUR EXISTING STAFF TO DO YOUR OWN PR

This option is great if you really want to retain complete control, as you can effectively work alongside the PR person of your choice, handing jobs and tasks over as you go.

It's also the most cost effective.

But consider how you delegate. Thrusting PR responsibilities on someone who is completely shy, or just didn't bargain for it when they joined, can be counterproductive. It has to be seen as a way forward for your staff and a way for them to learn more skills, rather than just to be landed with more work.

You will have to chose the right member of staff and present it to them in the right way. Ideally, the person you choose should:

- Be confident and able to think for themselves.
- Be aware of the media and read newspapers and magazines – i.e. be media savvy!
- Know your business well enough to represent it.
- Be clever enough to know when to talk and when to keep quiet.

The essential steps of handing over PR tasks are:

- Decide what you are going to hand over. Write their job description down and be very specific. If you still want to write all your own press material make sure they know this. If you want them to be responsible for chasing up interviews to find out which issue they will appear in and provide any photos and logos that are necessary, then make sure that they have this responsibility written down too.

- Make sure that they know your PR goals. Ensure that you are both starting from the same point and both have the same destination in mind. What is the aim of your PR – highly targeted info pieces in specific trade magazines or a general raise your profile campaign? Make sure you both agree on the end goals.

- Make sure that they fully understand what you want the public perception of your company to be. Write it down and make sure that every member of staff, and not just PR people, understand your vision. This is a good exercise in itself.

- Give them support. Everyone in your company and all your press contacts should know of their new position and responsibilities. Take the time to announce it publicly to all your contacts.

- Resist the urge to butt in and give them some space to get on with it.

- Have regular reviews to oversee work and progress. You may want to have these close together at first and then spaced further apart as things become more settled.

- Praise, reward and give them some recognition (even financially if possible) when they do a good job.

- Give them help. Not just from yourself but offer to send them on training courses if they need to increase their skills and knowledge base.

If you are considering taking on a PR company or freelancer to carry on with your PR activities then take a look at our Using A PR Company section, under U.

Paula Gardner

H

HOOKS

Clients often ask me where they can find a list of special events and PR orientated weeks that they can hook into for their press. Valentines Day and Halloween are obvious ones, but the year is littered with more obscure ones that could potentially be great hooks for a press release.

There are some very expensive services that provide huge online diaries with regular updates but one of the best free ones that I've come across is Count Me In where you can access a whole year's events and even post up your own. More details here: *www.countmeincalendar.info*

HEATHER WARING

Heather runs WaringWell (*www.waringwell.com*), a coaching and training company specialising in all areas of career development. Here Heather talks about her success with large national publications.

"Working with our clients who may be individuals or organisations, we help them develop appropriate strategies for career progression whatever that might mean for them at the time. It can be re-invention, promotion, retirement, re-entry into the workplace, a new job etc.

"PR has included articles in the Crème section of the Times, the Daily Express, Daily Mail, local papers such as the Wharf, The Recorder group and the Newsquest group. Contributions to articles in Cosmopolitan, Glamour, B, Red magazine as well as a regular slot as a career coach in Cosmopolitan for a couple of years. I also wrote a career column in the Sunday Express and a general life coaching column for my local newspaper group which went out weekly to five London boroughs. I was involved in three major life makeover projects for Cosmopolitan and still am featured as a career advisor for Fish4 jobs.

"Other PR has come through radio with slots on most local BBC stations, LBC, Virgin and Talk Sport and I have worked on radio campaigns with Virgin, Fish4 and the charity Victim Support to name a few. For other organisations and corporates I have been mentioned in brochures etc and wrote one on work/life balance and health for The Positive Food Company.

"Mind you, I don't spend as much time on PR as I should. Some of it is by default when asked to contribute to something but on average a couple of hours a month.

"I also talk to the journalists on my list to keep them updated. I also have built up some contacts with PR companies. I try and keep in touch with both groups regularly.

"I was doing some work with Fish4 who set up an event to meet with key journalists that they were trying to build stronger relationships with. One of the feature writers from Cosmopolitan was there and like the others did an article on me. She then came back and asked me to write a regular slot for them. It was that straight forward. Fantastic.

"Keeping on top of PR when things are busy is hard. I know I should spend more time on it but it gets knocked off the agenda.

"My highest point has to be writing the weekly column for the Sunday Express. Never did I think that I would write for a national newspaper. On the other hand I have spent time on what seems to be a good press release which seems to tick all the boxes and then no-one takes it up or even explores it further.

"What I've learned is that you have to keep at it. It pays to keep in touch with contacts and let them know what you are now doing. Also, you need to be inventive and different too and look at new ways of catching people's attention.

"When there has been an article or bit of PR about me I get new clients and other pieces of work. Writing a regular column also brought in clients who had been able to build a relationship with me through my weekly articles.

"My last bit of advice is to approach and ask. The worst that people can say is no. So, get out there and tell people all about you and your business."

Paula Gardner

I

INSPIRATION

It can be hard to come up with ideas and hooks, especially when it's press release time again, but here are some suggestions to get those creative juices flowing.

KEEP IT CURRENT

Keep up with what's happening in the news, whether it's by reading a daily newspaper, listening to a new talk show or keeping up with the Internet news. I don't mean just top headlines here - smaller news items, local and regional titbits can be just as rich in ideas. When you find something that you can tie in with your business use that topic as the starting block for your press release to bring it right up to the minute.

NAME DROPPING

Learn how to use the power of celebrities. We all love to read about celebrities and the press know that it's a great way hook in readers. So, keep an eye on what's going on in the celebrity land so that you, once again, can tie a press release into it.

PLAN AHEAD

Look at the calendar and take note of special days in the year. It's probably a good idea to avoid big occasions like Mothers day or Valentines Day, as you'll be competing with everyone else, but are there other smaller special days that you can use a hook?

INVENT AN OCCASION

Make up your own special days or even weeks - why not - everyone else does it. There's a fish and chips week, doughnuts week so why not a week of your choice!

SURVEYS

Look in the press for details of recently published surveys or do your own! *www.surveymonkey.com* is a great tool for setting up a survey and journalists often like press releases with some facts and figures in them.

EVENT

Make a public appearance and put together a release around that.

WHAT'S NEW WITH YOU?

Launch or revamp a product or service, or announce a new client win.

ILLUMINATION

Good, high quality images are a vital part of any PR campaign. They can humanise, show products to their best advantage, intrigue or amuse. A good photographer is a good ally to build into your team, and one worth investing in. Don't just think that having a digital camera or camera facility on your phone is enough.

One advantage to having good quality photos available is that you are more likely to get more space if you are covered and those photos are again more likely to draw the eye of the reader.

PRODUCT PHOTOS

The aim here is simply to illustrate the product, but of course, in the most attractive way possible. Keep the picture uncluttered with little or no background.

You can also produce photos of the product being used – say a new style hairdryer being used by a model. Here, you'll need a photographer skilled enough to highlight the product in action. Knowing your typical consumer is also going to be important. I once worked with a retirement coach (in her mid-thirties) whose website was full of white-haired old dears enjoying cups of tea. Although her PR and marketing efforts were bringing her visitors she wasn't having much success getting them to sign up for her newsletter, much less to go ahead and have coaching. As an independent observer I could see at first glance that anyone nearing retirement would be put off by these images. After all with a glossy Jane Fonda advertising skin cream on the TV and a 50 year old Madonna still dancing around in her leotard, people in their 50s and 60s today expect a very different campaign to what they might have had 20 years ago. One simple step of changing the pictures to make the whole idea of retirement much more aspirational worked. And with the many photo libraries around (more on that below), it didn't cost the earth either.

PEOPLE PHOTOS

If you are using a photograph of you in the campaign, once again it's best to enlist the help of a professional.

After all, no journalist really wants to see a photo of you in your shorts on holiday in Malta (I have seen it happen!) Once again, think about the image you want to portray. Is it serious, fun loving, or experienced? Remember, even the most serious of businesses can benefit from photos that show some personality.

You may need to talk to a few photographers before you find the right one, whichever style of photography you are after. Ask to see their portfolio, or check out the gallery on their website if they have one.

PHOTO LIBRARIES

There are many of these on the internet, such as *www.dreamstime.com* or *www.fotolia.com*, where you can download photos in different resolutions which you can use for campaigns, websites etc. In many of them you pay for credits upfront and then download photos as you need them.

FORMATS

Photos tend to come in high resolution (necessary for print) and low resolution (much easier to send via email). As it can be confusing at the best of times, I've asked the Do Your Own PR graphic designer, Kelly Molson of *www.rubbercheeese.com* to give us the low-down on exactly what you'll need for a PR campaign.

Kelly, what's the different between high and low resolution?

"High Resolution means any image that is the correct resolution for printing, usually 300 dpi or more. Sometimes called hi-res for short.

Kelly Molson
www.rubbercheese.com

"File formats can be PSD (Photoshop document) JPEGs (Joint Photographic Experts Group) & TIFF (Tagged Image File Format).

"Low Resolution is any image that is below the proper resolution for printing. Low-res images are usually 72 dpi, but can be anywhere below 200 dpi. Low-res images will not be the correct resolution for printed documents and often print poorly.

"File formats can be JPEGs, GIFs (Graphical Interchange File Format) and BMP (Bitmap)."

Which formats are best for publications?

"Jpeg or Tiff files are usually the best for publications, as long as the Jpeg files have not been taken from a website as they will have been optimised for Web use not print.

Which ones (high or low res) are best for a PR campaign, or would you need both?

"I'd suggest having both as you may be involved in PR offline and online! If you can supply your designer with the Hi-Res files, they will be able to convert them to Low-Res for you too."

What's the best way to get photos to a publication?

"I would never email large files unless the publication states you can. If the files are over 2/3 megabits some email systems can slow down.

"If you have the time you can send them on a CD but we find the quickest way is to use an online service called You Send It (*www.yousendit.com*).

"You can open a free account and send the files via You Send It. The recipient then receives an email with a link to download the files from, saving their email system from being clogged up!"

JULIE WOODARD

The Moroccan food, beauty products and homewares from *www.maroque.co.uk* have been featured in BBC Homes, BBC Antiques, Period Ideas, She, House and Garden, Instyle, The Sunday Times, Saturday Telegraph, and The Evening Standard.

Read on to find out what works for Maroque owner, Julie Woodard.

"I aim to spend about six hours a week on all PR/Marketing activities. I would like to spend more, but spending six would be nice on a more regular basis.

"Articles work really well, even if people don't use the article straight away, they come back. Product emails are useful, as it keeps the awareness there (and once the list is done, it's fairly straightforward to send). Competitions are a relatively cheap way of getting yourself known and even better if you get the contact list of all entrants.

"Talking to the press is fine if I can get hold of them. I need to work on building relationships so they think of coming to me for anything Moroccan, foreign or exotic. But it takes time taken in getting hold of people. And sometimes they can be plain rude.

"I sometimes also find getting started hard. Faced with a big PR list, I can turn procrastination into an art form.

"My highest point so far PR-wise has been having House and Garden phone up and say they would be using a part of my article I sent to them about four months earlier. And could they have the products to photograph? I was definitely on a major PR high that day; I could do anything.

"The first time phoning beauty editors was awful though, I had no idea people could be so rude. I have since watched the film The Devil Wears Prada, and I'm sure I spoke to several of them. It took a while and Paula's Talking to Journalists Course to regain the confidence to pick up the phone to them again.

"I strongly believe PR had had a very positive effect on increasing my turnover. I set myself a target turnover to achieve in a set period, spending the time and money on PR and I far exceeded my target and even my expectations.

"It is most definitely worth putting the time into PR. But get the right support; it makes your time more productive. To me, help and guidance are essential."

JUNK MAIL

You've spent a day on the release, honed it to perfection, sourced some great pictures, pressed send and then it speeds out into the world and ends up as junk mail or spam, in over half of your press list's inboxes. Not the scenario you wanted is it?

And the fact that most journalists work for large organisations that will have their own spam filters and firewalls may make it even harder not to fall into the trap.

Whilst I don't think you can ever make your email 100% safe from being marked down as spam, here are some suggestions that I have come across to help ensure that your email reaches the inbox of the person you intended. Whether they read it or not is another matter...

- Spam email filters and junk email traps do not declare their rules, and they are always changing, but you can start off by looking at your own spam filter and trying to work out what made those emails end up in it.

- Definitely avoid terms like free and cheapest.

- A personal "Hi Fiona...etc" at the beginning, with an even more personal sentence to follow might help.

- Make sure you have an unsubscribe option on your list. Most online database providers (like Constant Contact) have these already.

- Indeed, with Constant Contact you can actually assess your email and see its spam rating and how likely it is to fall foul of spam detectors.

- If you're sending it out from a personal account send it to a few trusted friends or colleagues to see if it reaches their inbox first.

- Keep contact regular but not overbearing. Daily emails are too much, unless it's to a group that has specifically signed up for them.

- I know that when I did my newsletter in text format it reached a lot more people. It seems that spam filters are often triggered by things like logos, formatting and photos. So, if you are doing a HTML newsletter or press release I'd suggest trying to keep it as clean as possible.

- You can post it online and send the recipients a short message with a link telling them to click here for the latest news. Whilst this may work well with a newsletter list, I'm not sure it would be a great idea for press, unless they specifically knew your name and would click out of curiosity.

- Leave off the attachments. If you've got great photos tell them to email you for them or post them online where they can download them in the format they need.

Finally here are some of the warning bells that one spam filter looks out for:

- Body of message incorporates a tracking ID number
- Body of message contains a large block of hexadecimal code
- Body of message contains one or more lines of "YELLING" (i.e., all-caps)
- Message includes Microsoft executable program
- Message body has at least 70 percent blank lines

- Message header indicates message was sent directly from dynamic IP address
- Message From field appears to not contain a real name
- Message From field ends in numbers
- Message header contains numbers mixed in with letters
- Message subject includes the term "offer"
- Message to: field contains spaces
- Message Reply to field is empty
- Subject has exclamation mark and question mark
- Subject is ALL-CAPS
- Message subject starts with an advertising tag
- Message From: field contains the term "friend"
- Subject contains "As Seen"
- Subject starts with dollar amount
- Subject contains "Double Your"
- Subject contains "For Only"
- Subject contains "FREE"
- Subject contains "Free Instant"
- Message contains excessive images without much text
- Message body contains the term "nobody's perfect"
- Message body claims not to be spam

Err... of course, there's always the post.

Paula Gardner

K

KEEPING TRACK

By keeping track I'm referring to the huge amount of names, emails and contact details that are going to be coming your way.

There's no point even starting your PR unless you've got a database set up. After all, not everyone who comes to your website or makes an enquiry is going to be ready to buy and you need a way to keep track and keep in touch.

My own database has undergone various incarnations over the years; some of them very cobbled together ones! It started off with a simple Smartgroups (now defunct, but it was a bit like Google or Yahoo groups) where people can join a list and email each other. It then progressed to a custom built one that was part of my website. But when that started to regularly get a bug I moved to Constant Contact (*www.constantcontact.com*) and found that so much better. I wished that I had done it before.

You can customise your emails and there is a good choice of templates so there should be something to suit your website or brand image. But the best thing about it is that you can track people who click through. Apart from being lots of fun, it gives you an idea of what's stirred interest, and what hasn't.

Constant Contact isn't the only option like this out there. Many of my clients use *www.aweber.com* and I've also heard of a few who use *www.icontact.com*. Most of them have a free trial and I'd urge you to play around and make full use of this, until you find one that suits you.

I've now moved my press lists over to Constant Contact as, again, it's nice to be able to track interest. However, I also have my press lists set up in Excel so it's easy to click on a contact and write an individual message to them.

One past client that has taken their database to a new level of sophistication is business introducers *www.sistersnog.com*. The business began as a branding consultancy, Snog The Agency, but when it started to incorporate networking get-togethers as part of its business strategy it needed a new database to make the process smoother. Sister Snog founders Hela Wozniak-Kay and Annie Brooks came up with the clever concept of extending their brand to their own database (as should only be expected from brand experts).

They now have a number of databases. One is cool virgins. These are interested women who have self-referred or been referred by someone else, but haven't, as yet, been to an event.

Hot Virgins are prospects who have been to an event and are now moved onto a 7 day action list which means that they have to decide whether to join, or not, within a 7 day window. Hela admits that it does sound quite severe, but it's acted as a great business strategy as it means that the people that do join are decision makers – movers and shakers – and it's precisely those people that she sees as the future of Sister Snog.

Once prospects join (if they don't decide to join then they are removed from the list, permanently) they become Sisters and receive more personal messages. As Hela puts it, "they are taken into the inner sanctum of Hela and Annie".

There are also Step Sisters (public figures who help attract members), Big Sisters (long term members) and, coming in the future, Twin Sisters, who will bring Sister Snog to other capital cities.

Although I have my general newsletter, I was inspired by Annie and Hela and created a separate (but less regular) newsletter for clients and customers, called Building the Buzz. Already, with its reservoir of warm leads who have previously worked with me, I can see that it's been worth doing.

KAREN THORNE

Karen Thorne runs *www.shropshirebreakfast.co.uk*. Like many of my clients, Karen and I have been in touch for years and I've watched her business grow and transform through hard work, experience and some good PR. Here are Karen's tops tips on how she did her own PR.

"I was working as a business coach and I received a grant from Women in Rural Enterprise to do some training. I decided I needed some marketing training and had met Paula through online networking and seen her courses so decided on the PR and Newsletter email courses. To be honest at the time I didn't really have a clue what PR was!

"I had always intended to open and run a B&B and after doing that very successfully for a couple of years, I decided to develop my coaching to be much more specific and set up Bed and Breakfast Academy.

"I started off by copying Paula's own idea and developed email courses for people who wanted to set up, market and run their own B&B. Since then I have gone onto run one and two day courses for prospective B&B owners. And in September, we are running a pilot for a course on Marketing Your B&B - so in the space of a few years I've gone from not knowing what PR and Marketing were to training other people how to do it!

"I probably spend 2 or 3 hours a week on PR. With the nature of my businesses it's difficult to allocate a set period of time each week - you never know when you might be cleaning a room or cooking someone's breakfast.

"I write a regular blog on my B&B site, updating it 2 or 3 times a week. That is proving a great way of staying in contact with past guests and encouraging prospective ones to stay with us rather than at another B&B. People feel they know me before they've arrived.

"I write 2 newsletters - one for the B&B and one for the training about once a month. My training newsletter has proved a great success. I have a sign up box on each page of my website and have grown my distribution list to about 1000 subscribers in under a year. I've discovered that people may find my website but not want to sign up for training straight away, but by sending a regular newsletter with hints and tip and details of new courses I remind them that I'm there. I've now started to get course bookings from people who signed up a year ago.

"When guests stay at the B&B I give them the option of opting into my B&B newsletter (they can also sign up on the website). I describe what it's like in Shropshire at the moment and let them know about suggested day trips and upcoming events. I get 2 or 3 repeat bookings as a result of each newsletter - it's just a case of gently reminding people you're there and showing them what they can do here on a second (or in some cases 10th!) visit.

"I've written some articles and included them on my training website. I noticed an increase in the number of people signing up for the newsletters and free courses since doing that. By writing articles you are demonstrating your expertise and giving people the confidence to buy your product.

"My approach to press releases is a bit ad hoc to be honest. I'll get a burst of energy, fire one off and then get discouraged if I don't hear anything.

"Another thing I do is keep an eye open (I use Google alerts, which emails me whenever Shropshire is mentioned on the Internet) and piggyback on other people's PR. For example, we have a wolf sanctuary near us that is on TV every few months. When I spot something like this I'll immediately update my website and newsletters so that people searching for the wolf sanctuary see my website in Google. I've had quite a few bookings as a result of this particular strategy.

"I also create PR opportunities in the business - such as entering the B&B of the Year Awards, which we won for the West Midlands last year. Whilst it's nice to have the award the main reason I do it is for the associate PR. "I'm gradually building up a list of contacts but this is my weak area. If I see someone I know getting national coverage I'll ask them to forward on contact details to me. I know the editor and deputy editor of a couple of well known glossies and make sure that I drop them a regular chatty email telling them what I'm up to and just reminding them I'm still here! I'm also contacted fairly regularly by production companies looking for prospective B&B owners so I always add them to my contact list.

"I do quite a lot locally. I've been featured frequently in our local newspapers and a couple of times on local radio.

"My highest point PR wise is when I sent off a press release to the deputy editor of Country Living magazine. I'd been lucky enough to find myself behind her in the lunch queue at a WiRE conference. The day she received my letter she emailed me and said she wanted to come on my course and review it for the magazine! The course review appeared in the June 2008 edition of the magazine and it was highlighted on the front cover. My phone didn't stop ringing for a month and I've filled 4 courses from it.

"They're also going to be featuring a review of my B&B in a later issue - so I'll have benefited from it twice.

"I had a very nice 2 page spread in the NFU Countryside magazine in May and have received quite a few bookings through that. That time the editor came to me as a WiRE member - so it pays to keep networking!

"Mind you, if I send off a press release and don't hear anything I get very discouraged.

"For me PR is a combination of lots of different things; newsletters, blogs, networking, press releases, article writing. I think the key thing is to be consistent and not give up and become discouraged. I also think you need to be on the ball and check out latest trends.

"One thing I have learnt is that you have to keep working at PR. As soon as the next edition of the magazine or paper comes out you're last month's news!

"I initially told Paula there was no way I would never do radio and TV. I've now done several radio interviews and had a tiny slot on News 24!

"All my newsletters, blogs and articles are gradually building up my business. However for a quick boost to your business you can't beat appearing in a well-known glossy! My Country Living Article is proof of the power of PR."

Paula Gardner

L

LEARNING TO READ

The Independent Media Section (on Mondays) recently ran a collection of interviews with journalists on what they thought about PRs and their techniques. Apart from hating it when people phoned up just to check if they'd got the release, their pet gripe was being approached by people who really hadn't bothered to read the publication.

This is a clear signal that we need to know what we're talking about before we pick up that phone but, with all those media opportunities out there, how do you find time to suss them out, and what are you looking for?

- Break your target publications down - a magazine a week, a niche a week, whatever you feel is realistic and not daunting.

- Build reading into key times of the day - during your train ride, or over a cappuccino first thing in the morning for instance.

- Read it twice - once for content and once with a PR eye.

- Analyse each publication – who would read it? For instance you may find that one food magazine concentrates on providing good hearty recipes and tips for family cooking, whilst another concentrates on gourmet products and cooking advice. Likewise, one runners' magazine may focus on running for health and fitness, whilst another is more geared to helping you run marathons.

- Read more than one copy of each publication.

- Follow individual journalists and what they write.

- Subscribe in advance so there's no excuse for not getting round to buying a copy.

- If you work in a team share out responsibility for titles between you.

LOCAL PRESS

There are some businesses that don't need to focus on national PR at all. For them, the local press is much more important. If you're one of those take note of my tips for getting press coverage locally.

Be aware that that some local papers exist only because of advertising and you just won't get in them without paying for it. If you do find this don't waste your time on them any more. Make a decision on whether it's something that you do want to invest in and advertise, or just concentrate your efforts elsewhere.

Getting involved in community affairs is a great way to meet the people who know the press, as well as the press itself. Offering sponsorship for fêtes, joining in local fun runs, joining the events committee for a local hospital – all these may bring you in contact with people from local publications.

Don't forget often overlooked local press opportunities such as the local Chamber of Commerce publication, or NCT (National Childbirth Trust) newsletter for female or parenting orientated products.

Build up contacts with a local press agency that may be able to help.

Play up the local angle in the press release.

Is there something going on nationally that your story can illustrate on a local level?

Don't be snobby. Even the local freesheets can be a great source of publicity – and ten years time that writer you contact at the freesheet could be writing for The Guardian.

One example of a way to interest local press is from Brighton based band Anemo (*www.anemo.co.uk*). Lead singer Hazelle Woodhurst used to be a bit-part actress and was in, among other things, Eyes Wide Shut. The band put out a press release about this and ended up with local paper coverage beginning "I was in an Orgy with Tom Cruise". With local press always looking for a story as a reason to give coverage to local acts, an association with a Hollywood star fitted the bill. As keyboard player Kingsley Sage says, "We did dine out on that one for quite a while!"

Paula Gardner

M

MEDIA REQUESTS

Media requests are basically requests for case studies and experts sent out by journalists. They send them to people with large groups of contacts (such as me!) and ask them to pass them on and suggest appropriate people, or they sometimes post them on relevant forums on the net.

Media requests tend to fall into two categories.

First we have the general request that doesn't have a deadline. Here's a real life example:

"I have recently begun to compile and write three consumer pages in Essentials magazine, a monthly glossy aimed at women aged between 30 and 55, many of them busy mums who like the magazine because it doesn't focus on celebrity or unattainable luxury items and clothes.

"My remit for Essentials excludes: food and drink, fashion and luxury fashion accessories, cosmetics, personal health and environmental issues - although I will very occasionally be able to look at certain things that come under these headings where a consumer test with a reader family would work well on my three pages, or where a special offer brings them within a 'get it free or get it cheap' or a readers' offer slot.

"I deal with everything else that goes into the everyday running of a household, from the pets to the school run, from insurance to the Internet, from carpet-cleaning to holiday-planning. We're looking for the really practical, yet slightly offbeat stuff - for example, we've recently had pieces about putting delicate glassware in the dishwasher and about silent alarm clocks and other non-shocking methods of getting woken up on time. We're always looking for ideas that smack of sensible, thrifty or clever shopping - but these items must be both useful and of good quality."

The above is a request from a journalist that wants people to keep feeding her ideas to hopefully inspire and fill her articles. So, the best way to use this request would be to get hold of the magazine (with no deadline, there is time) and come up with some ideas that would be relevant and send them over. Add photographs too, as you would have seen that the magazine is very visual. This will make your information stand out.

You could also add her to your media list if what you have to send is relevant. If your business is dentistry or gardening maintenance then there isn't much point.

Here's the second kind of request:

> "Childless women needed.
>
> "I'm still one case study short for an article I'm writing about women who are childless for a women's weekly magazine. Case study will be paid £150 and must be willing to be identified and pictured but it only involves a painless telephone interview ;-)
>
> "So if you know someone who might be suitable, it would be fantastic if you could forward their details to me or pass this request on and ask them to contact me ASAP, by Wednesday lunchtime, even if they just have any questions."

This request is for a specific article, with a specific deadline. You need to act quickly and get your response back as soon as possible. Once again, make sure you answer all the relevant info.

If you want to add her to a mailing list then my suggestion would be to drop her a line (after the article deadline has passed!), or call if there is a number specified and ask what sort of info she is after. It may be that she never covers any of your target publications or areas, in which case a quick call has saved you the bother of sending things out to her, as well as a barrage of useless emails for her.

But, if she does cover the sort of things or publications that could prove helpful, ask if she'd mind you sending her info occasionally. Most journalists say yes as it's often by being sent info and ideas that they come up with good article ideas that they can sell into publications.

The upside of media requests is that you know there's a need for something and if you can fill that, then great. The downside is that they do get a lot of replies to their postings, so it pays to be quick and persistent.

So, where to find these requests? As I've said, you can find them posted around the Internet or join our Divine Publicity Club and get them sent direct to your inbox.

N

NETWORKING

For many (especially service based businesses) networking can be *the key* to a thriving PR business. It's not PR in the strictest sense of the word, but as you are getting out there and publicising your wares and services I do think it is important that I include it here.

I have to say that I'm now in the lucky position of not having to go out networking as I get so many referrals coming to me. The turning point on this came when I had reached a significant number of people in my network. Some of these were on my *www.doyourownpr.com* newsletter, some were contacts I had made whilst setting up and running *www.chicklit.co.uk* and some were people I had met whilst networking at business events, workshops and conferences.

I probably spent about eighteen months doing serious networking, visiting at least five events a month and networking online. After that point I had enough experience to know which groups and meetings suited me and which ones were a waste of my time.

But the basics boil down to the more people you know and keep in contact with regularly, the more business will tend to get referred onto you.

Your time is precious, your budget limited (some of these networking events can be damn expensive and lunching out with contacts tends to hurt the old plastic if done too often)... so what's the answer?

FACE TO FACE NETWORKING

Let's think about strategic networking – where you are going to network and how much time and resources you will be devoting to it?

So, first off...

THINK ABOUT YOUR FAVOURITE CLIENTS

Where would they network and how would they do it? Via online forums, or organised business networking? Or is it more likely to be at HR conferences and exhibitions or even on the boards of charities or wine tasting or gourmet evenings? If you don't know, find out. Look at your target market and see if you know anyone – clients or friends or acquaintances - that fit into that category. Then ask them for their feedback and ideas. The larger the businesses you are after, the harder it is to meet them on a face to face basis and the longer it will take to see results.

WHAT WOULD THEY VALUE?

Are they more likely to value listening to you showing your expertise at a conference or business lecture, or would building up personal trust and credibility in a much more informal way be more effective?

WHAT RESOURCES DO YOU HAVE?

Do you work with anyone else so that together you can spread networking between you, or is it all down to you? How much spare cash do you have to spend on networking? Work out how much you are prepared to spend and think about how to allocate it wisely. I used to go to a lot of very small business events that gave free entry and inevitably the sort of people I'd meet would tend to be life coaches, alternative health practitioners, web designers and business coaches. Nothing wrong with that but they were either too small to afford PR or were after the same clients as me so I raised my game and paid to join groups where more established businesses tended to network. And, hey presto, I was talking to clients who could afford PR.

Again, how much time do you have? Start-ups tend to have more time to attend events but as you get busier you'll find it less and less easy to leave the office. It's vital to continue to build this into your business plan, even if you are happy being a one-person band and only want a few clients who will pay the rent and the annual holiday to Italy.

WHAT DO YOU ENJOY?

There's no point forcing yourself to weekly breakfast meetings if you're so stressed out by the effort you make getting there that you don't show off your best side. You will get the best results in environments and events that you enjoy. By all means try out a number of different events before you commit to paying any joining fees, but at the back of your mind think about whether this event is right for you long term.

How will you follow up your contacts? Will you be emailing them to say hello, or inviting them out for a coffee? Perhaps a phone call is better for you, or giving them an invite to something you've arranged or asking them along to something you are attending? Think about your follow up and what will feel comfortable for you. After all, meeting them is only half of the equation.

PUT TOGETHER YOUR STRATEGY

Plan your networking. How many events will you attend a month? How much time do you have you for follow up (emails/coffees/phone calls)? Does that mean that you'll be able to build up relationships with three people… or fifteen?

ONLINE NETWORKING

Many entrepreneurs find online networking particularly valuable, especially when they are starting out. It's often cheaper than going to events, doesn't involve transport and you can do it all from the comfort of your own home – even at two in the morning if the mood takes you.

Links back to your website from the postings that you make will also boost your status in the search engines and help more people find you!

Just like offline networking the keys to successful online networking are:

- **Decide on a Budget and Stick To It** -There are so many business and social networking opportunities out there, some of which require membership fees. Be savvy, most of them offer limited period free memberships to allow you to try them out so make the most of them.

- **Try Out a Few and then stick to the one/s you think will work for you** – and that you enjoy. I used to be a member of a very prominent business/social site and it brought me many clients but when people started competing for the bitchiest quips to people's posts, I decided to play down my activities there.

- **Don't Spend All Your Time Online** - This looks desperate and gives the impression that you have neither an interesting enough life nor enough work to keep you otherwise occupied.

- **Be Subtle** - It is not etiquette to push your business too obviously through online networking. The tradition is to receive by giving. So offering advice to businesses and joining in with a community is the best way to get known. Only start mentioning your business after you've made some valuable contributions, although for most sites it is OK to have your business details in your signature.

- **Be Persistent** - Make an effort to check the site regularly. One post a day is better than a flurry of activity at the weekend.

- **Treat Your Online Networking As You Would Offline Networking** - Never say anything derogatory about anyone, especially your competitors, and always remember that you are representing both your company and your current clients – anything you say is there for everyone to see!

TOOLS FOR GREAT NETWORKING

If you are investing your precious resources of time, energy and money into networking then having the best tools possible to do the job will help make your networking more effective. Here's our guide to what we consider the best networking kit.

YOUR ELEVATOR SPEECH

Put yourself in your fellow networkers' shoes. What do they want to hear? The answer is something that might help them.

Describe what you do, or your company does, in one easy to understand sentence that encapsulates it all in simple language. For instance I might say, "I teach small businesses how to do their own PR".

Now do the same thing but bring in the benefits to the customer. So, I might change my piece to "I show small businesses how they can use PR to get articles, features and interviews in the press and so raise their profile and attract more customers".

You'll probably notice that the first speech was all about me, what I do. The second is about what the other person can gain. The vital thing is to concentrate on the benefits you can offer them. Why don't you write your own elevator speech clearly outlining the benefits that your listener might find interesting?

YOUR ESCALATOR SPEECH

At some business events you may be called upon to give a slightly longer explanation than this and standing up there umming and ahhing doesn't do much for the reputation. Having your escalator speech handy and engraved on your mind is a clever networking move, and covers you for all those occasions where someone says, "That sounds interesting, tell me more" and you hadn't expected it.

Write your escalator speech, aiming for three, four or five short paragraphs. Concentrate once again on benefits not features.

For instance my talk goes like this:

"I show small businesses how they can use PR to get articles, features and interviews in the press and so raise their profile and attract more customers."

"They can choose a way to train that suits them, their business and their budget.

"At the end I guarantee that, if they follow the ecourse and plan I put together for them, they will get press coverage which will bring customers to them,

> eliminating the need for cold calling, and saving thousands of pounds on advertising or PR agencies."

Referring to a client that you recently helped get a lot of press coverage or new business is also a great thing to casually throw in as it gives you oodles of credibility.

Your turn now!

BUSINESS CARDS

Once the last word in networking, business cards are now increasingly seen as just another way to get your contact details across. We've had interactive CDs, postcards, mirrored cards, fluffy pink bunnies... what's next?

The essential rules of choosing a business card:

- Make sure that you never run out of them. If you are going for a template card at least choose something that fits in with your business - your company colours and your image.

- Keep your target market in mind. You may like young, fresh and funky but if your target market is golf courses then it might not be a grand idea.

- Stay away from those companies that offer you free cards in exchange for their logo on the reverse.

- Be a little different and add something extra to your card. It could be your elevator speech, a special offer that the owner of the business card can receive, the link to your free newsletter or perhaps even listing your services on the back. Make your card work for you in more than the most obvious of ways.

OPEN MIND

An open mind is your best tool - be receptive to new types of people, new conversations and new experiences.

ADMINISTRATION

When you get back write down a little (even if it is on the back of their cards) about the people you meet. In a few days you may well have forgotten who is who, and who you promised to call about that workshop date in April!

A practical filing system is also vital, whether it's having a specific drawer for your cards (as I do) that you sort through on a regular basis, or transferring them into a contact managing programme like ACT!, Outlook or the database of your Blackberry. Make it easy to keep in touch and keep on top.

A ROUTINE

I often find that after a networking evening people get in touch with me just at the same time I'm composing an email to them. You can tell that these are the experienced networkers. A brief (no sales) email saying something along the lines of "it was lovely to meet you" and some reference to your conversation is great and it keeps the lines open for further contact. Of course, if you got on like a house on fire, or had a huddled discussion about a joint venture that has got you both lit up with excitement, then by all means forge ahead!

THINKING OUTSIDE THE BOX

Think of networking as a martini.

It can be "any time, any place, any where" as the old advert goes. People put a label on networking and think that it only takes place at designated events, but in reality networking goes on all the time. There are opportunities to network at the school gates, at a party or salsa lesson. Being aware of this can help you be ready for it. Networking should become a natural part of your life.

It's not just about carrying a business card everywhere "just in case". It's an attitude, a realisation that the next person you meet might be a potential customer, or that contact you've been dreaming about for months.

Every time you leave the house or office you are selling and representing your business. Think of that next time you pull on your old gardening trousers for a quick trip up Tesco.

STARTING YOUR OWN NETWORK

Doing it yourself is an intriguing option. But it's not to be taken lightly. Once you organise something on an official basis you have responsibilities – other people who expect you to organise meetings on their behalf. You have to remind people of events, chase them up to confirm numbers and make a helpful little sheet full of contact emails so that everyone thinks they are getting the most from the event.

But I have heard of a few companies who have done it and found it a great reservoir of potential clients.

A MORE INFORMAL OPTION

Another alternative is to go through that list of contacts you are now gathering and offer to organise a one-off informal event. Making it small and intimate means that it's less hassle, you don't have to worry about booking venues and can relax and enjoy meeting the people you have invited. A good number is around 10 people as it's still intimate and yet big enough for attendees to think that they will be meeting some helpful people. And, yes, the biggest plus is that you can invite who you like, picking and choosing people that you would like to get to know.

Many business people are now aware that they should be out there networking to some extent. People may well appreciate the initiative that you've taken.

KEEP ASSESSING WHAT'S WORKING

Finally, I do believe that you have to look at your networking on a regular basis and reassess what's working for you and where you want your budget to be focused. You may find, as you grow, that your time is better spent on one to one meetings with possible (already very successful in their own right) strategic partners. In my opinion, the sooner you can get to this place the better, as this is where networking pays the most dividends.

Paula Gardner

O

ONLINE PR

PR is often thought to encompass just real life media such as newspapers, magazines and the web, but there's a whole world of online PR that needs attention as part of your business growth.

WHY ONLINE PR IS SO VITAL

Think about what happens when someone reads your name in a magazine or newspaper. Unless it's a household phenomenon such as Crown paints or Paris Hilton then chances are they've got to not only remember your name but also the web address too. I can think of countless occasions when I've come across a business' name in a magazine at the dentists waiting room or a friend's house, thought to myself, "I'll have to take a look at them I get back to the office," and then promptly forgot all about it.

Online PR and marketing promotion means that your name and website address is already in front of your potential customer. All they have to do is click on it. What could be simpler than that?

IT'S A VIRTUOUS CIRCLE

Write more articles, get mentioned on more websites, and you'll attract more people to your site. Get more people coming to your site and you'll be more likely to appear higher in the search engines when people search under your keywords and phrases. How cool is that?

YOU CAN'T GET MUCH CHEAPER THAN THIS

In the world of business promotion, online PR and marketing is as cheap as it gets. No investment in designing funky brochures, no paying out for high quality and expensive stationery, or exorbitant postage charges. A quick email accompanied by the relevant documents – press release, photographs, articles etc – followed up with a phone call. All it needs is your time – a small investment for such a potentially huge return.

EASY TO TRACK

Whilst it's hard to know who came to your site through what article and which offer in traditional media, tracking online PR and marketing is easy. If you've access to your web statistics you should be able to see the addresses of the sites where people are coming from – and watch how those figures correspond to the efforts you are putting in. And, on that note…

YOU CAN ALSO SEE WHO'S BUYING

If you're getting a lot of clicks from one particular site but no one's buying, you can take a look at why. Are they clicking through on a message that doesn't really convey what you are selling? Equally, the sites where people are coming to you and buying are the ones that need your attention. Look at ways that you can strengthen your association with appearances on these sites through news items, articles, competitions, postings in the forums, comments in the blog etc – and also look for other similar sites where you might achieve the same level of success.

RUNNING AN INTERNET PR CAMPAIGN

Kick it off with some market research to find out what sites your current clients visit, or get a student or Virtual Assistant to do some research on your behalf. Check your website's statistics - where are people coming from? This could even be other from people's commercial websites; it doesn't have to be a traditional publication.

If time is short decide what you will concentrate on. Perhaps it will be articles - offering them to other people's sites, online publications and syndication sites.

Or maybe competitions, which are great for building interest in a particular product. If you manage to get the entrants' details you can email them with a "sorry you didn't win but here's a special offer for you".

Post your press releases on press sites such as *www.pressbox.co.uk* or *www.prweb.com* (a small fee) and get them off to target online publications.

Set up your own blog. It's worked spectacularly for some of my clients and you can easily set up a free one at *www.blogger.com* in less than half an hour.

Comment on other people's blogs. Include a link back to your own site - great for search engine optimisation too.

Have a newsletter in place so if people come to you but aren't ready to buy there's at least something you can offer them.

95

Get into Social networking - whether it's Ecademy, Facebook, Bebo or whatever, the trick is to choose one and do that properly rather than half hearted attempts on a number of sites.

Have plenty of content on your own website - articles, case studies, think pieces - the more the better. And, and the more often they are updated, even better!

Whatever you put out, make sure that it contains the right keywords for your business and keep putting new content out regularly. This is one area where quantity will really make difference.

I also love the way that the web is so much more instant than traditional publications. You can update your website almost instantly (if you have a content management system that is. If you're still relying on a web developer to fit this in for you then you need to rethink this). You can post up a press release in a day and if one of your articles goes on a syndication site it can quite possibly be seen by millions of people.

LIVENING UP YOUR WEB CONTENT

The more you have to offer to go with your copy, the better, think about...

- Photos - of you, the product, a case study, whatever.
- Your logo.
- A resource box of helpful info that people will appreciate.
- A blurb - who are you and what can you do for your customers.

Remember that web copy is different to offline copy. Articles are much shorter and broken up with headings, paragraphs and bullet points. I prefer them to be around 500-600 words max as I know that most people find it hard to read anything longer than that from a computer screen.

OPEN EVENTS

If you regularly run workshops, take a leaf out of Audrey Boss's (see A) book and keep a press place free. Then a few weeks before the event, send around an invite to your press list (or selected names from it). I always find it best to target people who have previously shown an interest, or at least taken time to speak to me. If you don't get any joy from this, follow up with a phone call.

If you have premises that may be worth a visit, such as a retail outlet, then arranging an annual press open day is an easy to adopt PR activity. Julie Woodard from *www.maroque.co.uk* runs a yearly open day where she invites both press and public to her showroom to sample Moroccan food, listen to music and enjoy a guided tour around all the goodies therein.

If you don't have a showroom or premises consider holding an event, or partnering up with another business to hold a joint event. I've often managed to get room hire at lovely bars and nightclubs for free if I chose a Monday or Tuesday. Yes, even in central London. Or look for an art gallery that would like some publicity – if you can get press along then that's quite an incentive for them to partner up with you.

So, what should you do to keep the press amused and interested? It can range from low-key drinks and networking, to a full presentation. Obviously, each business will showcase their talents differently.

Oh, and don't get forget goodie bags. I have stepped in and rescued more than one event by getting in touch with other companies who want to reach the press and asking them for goodies we can include in a goodie bag. And it's a nice touch to email a journalist who has said "yes" a little reminder that "we have your personalised goodie bag waiting for you".

P

PR BUDDIES

A PR buddy is someone who, just like you, is aiming to get press coverage. It helps if you have similar target markets, as you can swap information, but even if you don't you can still get a lot from the relationship. The trick is to find someone who has a similar size business and that you feel you'll enjoy working with. Don't be shy, just come out and ask them!

Once you've agreed to buddy up, here are some suggestions on how to take it further:

- Find a time when you've both got an hour to spare and book it into your diary.

- Revisit each other's websites.

- Put together a vision for your business and what you'd like to achieve with your PR and then swap visions.

- Split your call into two half-hour segments and then each person can go through their goals.

- Each buddy should consider what they'd like to achieve PR wise – try to focus on a small number of easily definable goals, e.g. I'd like to get articles published in the parenting press or I'd like to increase my newsletter subscribers to 5000.

- Decide what actions you could take to meet the goals (and the other person can chip in with ideas here).

- Work out what you commit to doing in the next month or six-week period (however far apart you decided you'll have your calls).

- Finally, determine what you'd like from the other person e.g. for them to read through your press release or email you on 17th to check that you've approached 5 editors with ideas for articles.

It's a formula that can take you through your first few calls, after which you'll probably find your rhythm and you'll also know each other's big goals so you don't have to go through those all over again.

HOW TO GET THE MOST OUT OF YOUR CALLS

The relationship will work best if you:

- Are honest about what time you can give from the beginning. Don't give your buddy unrealistic expectations.

- Are in balance, the more you give the more you'll get out of this relationship.

- Tell the truth. If something is badly written or just plain uninteresting have the courage to tell the other person. It may be a little awkward at first but in the long run they'll only appreciate you for it.

- Keep the fun. Yes, work is the focus k
  time to find out what makes each
  make it much more fun for you an
  likely to actively look forward to and enjoy the call.

PRESS RELEASES

The Ten Most Frequently Asked Question About Press
Releases...

1. WHAT IS IT AND WHY DO I NEED A PRESS RELEASE ANYWAY?

A press release is more often than not a one-page sheet
that's sent out to press, either via email or post. It's
designed to catch their eye with some news or something
unusual about your or your business. Whereas years ago
all you had to do was send a press release out and you
could be pretty confident that at least part of it would be
reprinted, today that's very unlikely.

Nowadays, a press release is more of a tickler -
something that alerts the journalists to what is going on
in your business. If it's of interest they'll follow it up
and more often than not write their own piece or use a
snippet of yours inside a larger piece.

2. CAN'T I JUST HAVE ONE PRESS RELEASE AND KEEP USING THAT?

Press Releases are meant to be about news - either
something that's happening within your organisation,
or something that's happening out there in the world
that you can tie a story to. A stale release that gets used
again and again is going to get noticed... and for all the
wrong reasons.

That's not to say that you can't use some of your material in each release. The information on you and your business - how and why it started - will probably stay fairly stable, which means that you can re-use that and pour your energies into creating something eye-catching and compelling for the first few paragraphs.

3. WHO DO I SEND THEM TO?

You can buy lists from organisations like *www.romeike.com* (but it's not cheap), you can make up your own with The Guardian Media Directory and a few days work, or you can get us to put one together for you. But nothing beats actually looking at the publications yourself and working out which parts of a newspaper or magazine are right for you. And don't just buy one copy - start reading a few and get a feeling for language, target market and what you have that will suit it.

You rarely send things to the editor (unless the publication is very small). It will probably be the features editor, news editor or perhaps a shopping, homes, health or women's editor. Remember that nothing works as well as reading the publication to see who's who. And, even then, you'll need to pick up the phone to find out if they are still there (vital in a publication that could have been written 4 months previously) and their correct email address.

4. HOW DO I SEND THEM - POST OR EMAIL?

When I first started in PR we didn't have email, only a fax machine. I used to spend one day a week just standing by the machine and faxing... faxing... faxing... and at least one other day stuffing envelopes.

We don't have to do that any more and that's great. But the problem is that everyone else can email too and journalists often get one hundred plus emails per day in their inbox. No wonder it's hard to get yours to stand out.

Again, if you've got great photos, putting them into an email might look good but may get your email blocked by a firewall and presumed to be Spam.

So, if you've got anything visual - where people need to see the photos to go "wow", I suggest that you both email and post your release. It may cost more but it will be increasing your chances considerably of getting it seen and read.

Information type releases can be just emailed, but remember, keep everything in the body of the email (say photos etc are available by request) and follow up with a call.

5. HOW OFTEN SHOULD I BE SENDING OUT A PRESS RELEASE?

Large companies like L'Oreal or ICI may be sending out a number each month, but for smaller businesses once a month or every six weeks is a good goal to aim for.

The best way to go about this is to block press release days into your diary, where you write up your release (or commission someone to write it for you) and get it out to the press. If you glance at your diary and see that one is coming up more likely than not your subconscious will get to work and by the time you've sat down at your PC it will have come up with some great ideas.

6. SHOULD I INCLUDE SOME QUOTES?

The answer is yes, but it's much better if they are not from you - unless you are imparting some vital information or bits of advice.

What doesn't go down well with the press are business owners who ramble on about how fabulous their product is, or how excited they are. They don't care!

What the press does like are customer sound-bites or, even better, third party experts and celebrities. So, get your thinking hat on and ponder whom you know…

7. OKAY, I'VE SENT IT, WHAT NEXT?

Wait 2-3 days and then get on that phone. It's often by speaking to the press that you galvanise them into reading the release in the first place. If you possibly can it's worth rounding something up that you can then send onto the press as a next step (after enquiring by phone if they'd like to receive it first). This could be a sample, review copy, invitation to a press event or just some ideas for articles that you could put together for them.

8. I CAN'T REALLY BE BOTHERED. CAN'T I JUST PHONE THEM AND HAVE A CHAT?

Yes, you can, and it's great that you're prepared to do that. But even if you charm the pen into their hand they'll still want to see a press release and better to have one already written and to hand than to have to conjure one up under pressure.

9. CAN I SEND IT TO MORE THAN ONE PERSON AT THE SAME PUBLICATION?

Yes, yes, yes. That's common practice and no one will raise an eyebrow as long as you target well and don't bother people with things they don't cover.

10. CAN YOU SHOW ME SOME RELEASES?

Yes, take a look at the Extras section at the back of this book.

PERSISTENCE

Let me tell you a story. Now and again I sometimes, for very special clients, do PR, as opposed to teaching and training on the subject. And for the past three months I've been contacting this features editor of a well-known and high profile magazine. I can't say she's been a delight to talk to, as at times she's been intimidating and always, always gives out "I'm busy" vibes.

But this week she actually called me when she'd finally had time to look and digest the bits and pieces I've been sending her. We're now going ahead with something but the whole process has taken at least three months - and involved me phoning or getting in contact in one way or another at least once a week.

That's very nice you say, but why is she telling me this? Well...

It shows that perseverance is important.

It Illustrates that however busy or aloof a journalist can sound it is still worth persevering as long as they don't give you an outright no.

It's a cautionary tale of how long the process can actually take.

If you flick through this book and look at the case studies I've included you'll see that almost all of them talk about the importance of persistence and not giving up. See, it's not only me!

PODCASTING

Alan Stevens
www.mediacoach.co.uk

Podcasting is an oral broadcast that's recorded and later downloaded and listened to on a PC or through an MP3 player or IPOD. It's a tool that media coach Alan Stevens (*www.mediacoach.co.uk*) has been using for years, although he has recently re-branded his Podcasts as the "Media Coach Radio Show" and subsequently got many more downloads as a result. Interesting.

Alan uses his weekly ezine as the basis for his radio show, adding a theme tune, voice-overs and structuring it just as one would a radio show. Alan explains, "My inspiration was Alistair Cooke's Letters from America. I used to listen to them for years and marvelled at just how professional and interesting they were. There was not one word that was out of place or wasted. Wonderful."

Alan's got some great how-to advice on how to actually do a Podcast, which I'm reproducing with his permission here.

PODCASTING - A SIMPLE HOW-TO-DO-IT GUIDE

Podcasting is a simple and effective way to deliver your message to people around the world. In essence, it is the creation of an audio file, which is then uploaded to a website. The file can be downloaded to PCs or portable MP3 players (often iPods, hence the name of the game). The real beauty of podcasting is that people can subscribe to your podcast, so that every time they plug their MP3 players into their PCs (a process known as synchronisation), they receive the latest version of your podcast.

In order to podcast, you need:

- A PC with speakers and microphone
- Sound recording software
- A website to host the podcast
- A way of promoting your podcast

Here's my advice for each of the elements.

A PC WITH SPEAKERS AND MICROPHONE

Of course, you probably have one of these already, but I'd advise buying a headset with attached microphone. It's easier to use and provides a better sound quality. The equipment simply plugs into the speaker and microphone sockets at the back of your PC. The cost is around £20 to £30 and they are available from any computer store. If you pay a little more you can get a switched version so that you don't have to unplug and replug if you want to use your PC speakers.

SOUND RECORDING SOFTWARE

There's lots of this around and you can buy very sophisticated editing packages. I like to keep it simple, so I use Audacity (*http://audacity.sourceforge.net*). It is easy to use and free, so gets my vote. If you use it to create MP3 files (a good idea), then you need another piece of free software called the LAME Encoder. Both are available at *http://audacity.sourceforge.net/download/windows* (unless you have a Mac, in which case the software is at *http://audacity.sourceforge.net/download/mac*).

Simply download the software and allow it to create an icon on your desktop. To create your podcast click on the red button and start to speak. When you have finished click on the yellow button. To save the file click on File, then Export as MP3. Give the file a name and include your name and the podcast title in the pop-up window. Save the file.

A WEBSITE TO HOST THE PODCAST

You can host the file on your own website, but this may require you to do some work. If you don't mind spending five dollars a month you can use *www.libsyn.com.* I've used them for a while now and found them to be excellent. You simply create an account, log on and upload your podcast file. You can provide other details, such as a brief description and a logo. A page will be created (you can select a template for the design), from which people can download your podcast. For example you can see my page at *www.alanstevens.net/podcasting.htm*.

PROMOTING YOUR PODCAST

If you use a service like Libsyn.com, they will assist you to promote it to the major directories such as iTunes, iPodder and Podcast Pickle (honestly). In addition, you can search for podcast directories and submit your podcast directly. The process is very simple. Finally, mention your podcast whenever you can and provide links to it from your website(s). Encourage others to promote it too. Good luck.

My own foray into Podcasting has been to record my own teleclasses and send them to clients as an MP3 download – not quite as sophisticated as Alan's radio shows by a long shot, but free teleclasses have proven a great way to attract new and curious clients.

Paula Gardner

Q

QUICK, QUICK, QUICK

PR can be a funny thing. For ages you can feel as though you're pushing against nothing, sending things out to get nothing back, calling journalists and not getting through. And then something happens. You get an email with a query from your release; a journalist phones and leaves a message. It's happening and it's great.

What you need to realise is that you're not working in your time any more. You are in "press time" and that means that any queries or calls that you get need to be answered as soon as possible. If a journalist is looking for someone to comment on something and can't get hold of you they may leave a message, but if you haven't got back to them pretty pronto then you can bet they'll be moving onto the next person on their list.

It's vital to give press a mobile number that is checked regularly, and likewise make sure that emails are checked regularly, especially if a press release has just gone out. If you are working within a team make sure that everyone is briefed and understands what to say to the press and how to contact you.

I wouldn't advise giving press an answering service as a contact number. Whilst I'm sure there are some pretty good ones out there I haven't yet come across (from a caller's or user's point of view) any that I would be happy bringing into a PR campaign. You need to offer a much more personal option.

R

RESOURCES

At Do Your Own PR we're always on the look out for great (on a budget) resources to help with your publicity and here are the top ones we are always recommending to clients.

THE GUARDIAN MEDIA DIRECTORY

Published every year, this gives you a pretty comprehensive list of UK newspapers, magazines, radio stations and TV companies. It's now getting better and better with digital media too. Available from Amazon.

WWW.MEDIAUK.COM

This is along a similar theme but a free website. Not quite as good as the Guardian Media book, but enough to get you going.

WWW.EXPERTSOURCES.CO.UK

Here, you can register yourself as an expert in your field and watch the media requests come in. It's a site where journalists look for sources and radio and TV shows look for guests. One of my clients even got approached by CNN. The trick is to make yourself unique.

GOOD PR BOOKS

My first book *Get Noticed, How To Boost Your Business Profile In 30 Days Or Less* provides you with lots of actions and less theory that will really make a difference to your visibility. Other inspirational books that I've found useful are:

- *Guerrilla PR, How You Can Wage An Effective Publicity Campaign Without Going Broke*
  by Michael Levine.

- *101 Ways To Market Your Business*
  by Andrew Griffiths.

- *Media Training 101, A Guide To Meeting The Press*
  by Sally Stewart

- *PR Power* by Amanda Barry

READING HABITS

Read a daily newspaper every day (varying them) and, if your product or service is mass market, also a celebrity gossip mag once a week (e.g. Closer) to keep up with who's in and what stories are making the press at the moment.

ROBYN WEST

Robyn West founded *www.pogopack.co.uk*. I've probably known Robyn for three to four years now. She's a reluctant PR-er, but I have watched her get to grips with it and flourish.

"PoGo supports girls in the early stages of puberty with the PoGo Pack, a period starter kit for girls aged 8-14, together with information and resources on our website. The pack contains everything a girl needs to manage her periods: a selection of pads specifically for young girls, simple information, a period planner for tracking bleeding, a pull-out purse for daily use and ancillary products.

"The idea came about when my daughter was going on holiday. When I discovered that there wasn't an all-in-one kit available in the shops, I set about creating my own. It's a great time-saver for parents too. I know many mums will throw their hands up in horror at the idea of girls starting their periods as young as eight, but it's an increasing trend. I want to encourage parents to ensure their daughters are prepared for the unexpected.

"PoGo had a fantastic double-page feature in the local paper that resulted in lots of orders. I'm also pleased to have the full support of the School & Public Health Nurses Association (SAPHNA), which has been brilliant at spreading the word because they love what the PoGo Pack achieves.

"Until recently I haven't been spending much time on PR, but I've now blocked out one day a week to dedicate to PR activities because I know that it's the consistency that pays dividends. I've built up an extensive list of media that I want to target, and different industries and ideas to try.

"Getting publicity in the local paper generated a lot of interest. A local pharmacy ordered PoGo Packs for their four branches because their customers kept asking if they stocked them! I do lots of presentations to parents & girls at local schools, and that's great for creating awareness and getting sales. I offered the Girl Guides some PoGo Packs as prizes and that was a really worthwhile exercise, so I plan to repeat this with other publications.

"I'm lucky that people understand the benefits of my product immediately, so it's easy to talk about it, hence networking really works for me. This has resulted in Business Link wanting to use me/PoGo as a case study. I'm now making networking a regular part of my monthly calendar.

"One learning experience was working with the PR department of a large department store, which wasn't terribly successful, to be honest. The promised national PR campaign to launch the PoGo Pack was backed up with insufficient action, which resulted in zero publicity. The PR department has lots of brands to promote, most of which are far bigger and more exciting than mine. Getting hold of people when they have celebrity launches to organise is a challenge! Also, the in-store promotion I was involved with was a valuable learning experience, particularly when one store lost the stock. However, I managed to turn it to my advantage by thinking creatively.

"Something I don't like about PR is calling journalists on the big national publications, who are sometimes too busy. I feel like I'm being a nuisance, but try to keep reminding myself that it's not personal and to think about how I can help them. I also had unrealistic expectations of the department store - thinking they'd put PoGo on the map. Another dreadful moment was a networking event I went to that was heavily attended by men. Having them freeze in horror when I gave them the most sensitive elevator pitch I could think of was not something I wanted to repeat. I decided women's networking groups were the only route for me.

"But my highest point has definitely been the newspaper feature, which continues to generate orders months after the event because people have held onto it. Due to that feature, I was approached to enter the Ask About Medicines awards, which acknowledge excellence in communications with the public on health matters. The awards will be announced soon so it would be rather exciting to be short-listed.

"I have learnt that the best person to get out there and shout about my product is me and that any publicity is going to be down to my efforts alone. I've also seen the benefits of making that effort, and it's incredibly motivating, but the benefits are short-lived and it's making a constant effort that makes the difference.

"Every activity I've done so far has resulted in something positive, whether it's sales or invitations to participate in something else, which is equally beneficial to the business. I find word of mouth has been a very powerful tool for PoGo and I'm astonished where some enquiries come from.

"My final words of advice would be:

• High quality images are crucial for product-based businesses.

> • Start building a list of media to target and capture all ideas in one place, so that when you do set aside time for PR, you immediately have something to work on.
>
> • Make the most of opportunities when they arise. I subscribe to a few newsletters and have just sent off a pitch for a media call. Even if it doesn't amount to anything, it's one more person who knows about the PoGo Pack - who might tell someone else."

RADIO TIPS

Once upon a time going on the radio meant a journey to the station and sitting around until they were ready for you. Nowadays, it can more often than not be done down the phone line... sometimes even on a mobile. Quick, simple and easy - job done in minutes! Here are our suggestions on breaking into radio:

LISTEN

The shows with the biggest figures often tend to be morning/breakfast shows and drive-time, so I'd suggest listening to these first to get a handle on how your business might fit into the subject matter. But, really, the most important thing is to find the right show for you, whatever time it's on.

MULTI-TASK

You can listen to many shows (or a recording of them) on your computer as you work. No excuses like not having a radio!

PERSEVERE

Behind the scenes staff often work shifts, especially in the larger stations, so do be patient when trying to get hold of the right person. A deputy producer is always a good bet. If not, then try a researcher. You may have to approach a number of people on the same show to get through to someone who'll listen to your pitch.

GET TOPICAL

When approaching radio your best bet is make sure your story is topical and ties in with something in the news. Whizz off a press release on the theme of the day or just call or email telling them what you've got to say on the topic. If this is at all controversial, even better.

SHOW EXPERIENCE

If you've been on the radio before, mention it - especially if you are going for one of the national stations. If you've got a tape or MP3 recording of your appearance, mention this, as they may want to hear it.

DON'T GET CAUGHT OUT

For the best interviews assume that you're live as soon as you pick up the phone. You might well be. Don't presume that the host already knows what you do as the first time they hear about you may be a few seconds before the show. Be prepared to explain everything quickly and succinctly. Stand, rather than sit, when you are speaking if you possibly can, although in a studio that might seem a bit rude! Finally, keep to an even pace - not too slow, not too fast.

RESEARCH

If you are going into the studio ask what they want you to cover. Always ask beforehand if they can do you a recording of the show - later it might be too late!

JUST IN CASE

I always find it helpful to have my phone number written in front of me – it may sound stupid but I have heard people go blank and I wouldn't want that to happen to me.

OFFER VALUE

Be ready with lots of advice - often radio shows want you to impart good solid tips that people can put into practice straight away.

USE IT

And, when you've done it you may be able to add it as an audio clip (with their permission) on your website, or merely just say "as heard on BBC Radio".

Someone who had a great radio experience is Heather Waring of *www.walkerscoach.com*

"In June this year, myself and my East End Girls walking group were featured on Radio 4's Ramblings Programme. It's really heightened our profile and has brought in many new members for my walking group as well as requests to set up other groups throughout the country. It's also brought me new clients wanting to train for treks and others who want to walk and be coached at the same time."

Susan Heaton-Wright of *www.nsn-productions.com* also found herself on the radio recently:

"With regards the radio interview I was promoting a course I was running. However, I had the opportunity to start coaching one of the junior presenters in the studio; quite a challenge as there are microphones everywhere and I am normally very interactive with my clients. However, I was able to mention my course, showcase my expertise and I have been invited back. I have coached the young presenter and will be doing some more. She is recording the sessions to provide a regular progress report on how she is developing her speaking skills and voice. I am going to be invited back onto the programme to discuss her progress too. I have been able to put the recording of the interview on my website and it adds some credibility to my expertise."

Paula Gardner

S

SABOTAGE
THE 7 DEADLY PR SINS - HOW WE SABOTAGE OUR OWN PR!

Even with the best will in the world, there are ways that we sabotage our PR campaigns. Let's take a look at the common PR traps we all - even experienced PR people - fall into.

1. NOT MAKING TIME

Because PR is very much self motivated it's easy to put it to one side for that fantastic day when you don't have anything else to do. And we all know that that day never happens. You need to spend at least an afternoon or morning a week on PR to see results. Any less and it just won't be worth it.

Solution: Choose a few consecutive hours and mark them in your diary as PR time. Keep them sacred - just as you would do for a weekly exercise class - and let nothing interfere. It might take a while to see the results but they will happen, I can assure you.

2. FAFFING ABOUT

This is one trap that I see a lot of people fall into. At networking meetings I often hear phrases like "I intend to really get started on PR when I've finished tweaking my website"... and then three months later you meet them and they say the same thing. Or sometimes it's "I'm just about ready but first I wanted to have a chat with my business advisor, coach and accountant about my goals and then we'll put together an overall marketing strategy." Argh!!! Stop it! Websites can be tweaked as you go and, although consultations with professionals are important and valuable, there comes a time when you've just got to take that leap and do it.

Solution: Think Nike - just do it.

3. THE BIG SCARY PRESS RELEASE

For many this can be the biggest stumbling block that they'll come across and this is where their PR campaign comes to an end. Full stop. But the important thing to remember is that one press release isn't going to change the future of your business - it's the persistent drip, drip of getting your name and story out to the media that is going to do that.

Solution: Get someone else to write it, or try our Write Your Own Press Release ecourse.

4. NOT FOLLOWING UP

I know - you're busy. We all are. And it is perfectly possible to conduct a PR campaign without picking up the phone. But anything you do will be maximised by following it up and building up relationships with the press. Almost every one of my coaching clients who have admitted feeling anxious about doing that have all gone onto being able to do it without too much of a qualm. Some even experience a great buzz because they know that the results are well worth that anxious gulp just before they pick up the phone.

Solution: Start small - try your local papers or a small circulation magazine - and work your way upwards. Or you could try our Cold Calling Crash Course and get personalised feedback on your own technique.

5. FALLING INTO THE "I WANNA BE FAMOUS" TRAP

Yes, it is rather nice if Ideal Home Magazine wants to interview you about your new bathroom but if your business is actually running an IT firm then is it really that relevant? I'm not saying don't do these things if they come up, but use your active PR time to focus on getting coverage in publications and places that will actively promote your business.

Solution: Think carefully about who and what you need to focus on and keep to your list. Pin it over your desk to remind you daily if necessary.

125

6. NOT DOING YOUR RESEARCH

Contacting a publication that only runs celebrity stories with a press release on the launch of your cleaning business is a waste of both your time and theirs - unless one of your clients happens to be David Cameron or Madonna.

Solution: Look at your publications and the stories they currently run. If they like statistics and facts, get some from somewhere. If they like human-interest stories, see what you can do to tug their heartstrings with your own - or a client's - story.

7. BEING TOO SUCCESSFUL

The honey trap of PR! Good PR inevitably raises your profile and brings in new work but the danger is that you then don't have the time to continue with your PR activities, and then six months down the line things go quiet again.

Solution: You need to continue to set aside a regular time investment in PR - or, if things are really busy and you feel it's the right step to take - get someone onboard to do PR. It could be an outside agency, a freelancer or even one of your staff or a VA who is responsible for keeping some PR activity ticking over.

SHARYN WORTMAN

Sharyn Wortman runs a tea and philosophy business called *www.todaywasfun.com*. Sharyn did some PR coaching with me many years ago now. Since then her business has gone from strength to strength and I often spot her teas all over the place. In fact, business seems to be going so well that she does now use someone to help with PR!

"I started working with Paula in 2004. My business was just 2 and a half years old and I had three products in the range. At that stage I was still hand blending all my teas in my flat in Hampstead and distributing it all myself. I had a handful of loyal stockists and was on a mission to spread the word about what I was doing in order to increase the number of stores that stocked my product and to drive sales. It was just me and a whole lot of energy, dawn to midnight.

"Now we have over 250 stockists in the UK, including stores like John Lewis, Harvey Nichols and Harrods. We also supply our teas into Russia, Paris and numerous stores in Spain. I no longer blend the tea by hand and have it all warehoused down in Berkshire. We have won numerous awards including Best New Organic Product 2005/ 2006, Soil Association taste award, Gift of the Year award in 2005 and Best New British product in Paris 2006. Last year we were the first company to launch a carbon neutral food and drink product - Green Green Tea. Last month I took the big step of employing someone to work full time with me in the office along with another girl who works on sales 3 days per week.

"I put together a newsletter, Tomorrow's Soup, each month that usually takes a couple of hours. I now hire a PR consultant to work on a project basis when we have a new product to launch and need to generate PR activity. This works out at approximately 20 days per year.

"Developing my newsletter has been one of the best activities I took up. Each month it works to remind everyone that we exist and keeps them up to date with what we are up to.

"We also offer Harvey Nichols exclusivity when we first launch a product. This means that the product will receive a more dedicated PR push and they have lots of lovely press contacts that they deal with.

"For getting column inches however nothing beats good old fashioned getting on the phone and calling up the journalists, followed by sending through a press release, another phone call and then free product if they are interested enough to taste our teas or photograph them.

"The press love us. They are always ready to hear from us and add our new Tea & Philosophy range to their what's hot editorial pages. I am also starting to develop a profile in the business community too for my ideas on setting up and running a business a little differently. Did I tell you we all have Fridays off?

"Mind you, keeping a track and getting copies of all the coverage that we get is boring.

"Lydia Slater wrote about our Teastack in the Sunday Times Style magazine in October 2005 and the sales went berserk. One of our online stockists asked us to take her link off our website as she couldn't cope with the amount of orders that were filling up her inbox every day. It seems that the Sunday Times style magazine reader is our perfect customer profile and all our customers saw a huge demand for our Teastack which in turn drove huge sales for us.

"Being profiled in the Times magazine as an 'antipreneur' has been a high point. I finally felt like someone had recognised my achievements. Finally someone, other than my friends and family knew how long and hard I had been working. It was also quite fun when my fiancé and I appeared in the Financial Times How to Spend it Magazine. We both received emails and calls from all our friends in far-flung places like Singapore, New York and Johannesburg - we had no idea that the magazine was syndicated.

"Over the years I have learnt that you have to BE PERSISTENT, PERISTENT, PERSISTENT.

"Secondly you must make it easy for the journalist. Have lots of information, images and samples at the ready. Members of the press are either overworked or extremely lazy. I never know which. What I do know is that if you give them everything on a plate you make their job easier and the more likely they are to run your material, verbatim. I now have a page on my website that has all the press releases and images to upload, I send them a link if they're on a deadline and hey presto!

"I used to work in advertising and always advised my smaller, independent clients to start off their 'advertising' with PR campaigns. Readers and viewers will always believe something they read as editorial over something that appears in a paid advertisement. So don't pay for advertising space until you have a national brand and the retailers are demanding it.

"Try to establish a brand personality and tone of voice early on and stick to it.

"Make sure you put aside some dedicated PR time in the week, month. There is always something more urgent or distracting that is going to get in the way of chasing journalists on the phone. Make a commitment to an amount of time and stick to it, if you don't have time find someone who is good on the phone and pay them a couple of hours a week to call for you but do ask them to do it from your home/office. I did this 2 years ago and found that it is much easier for someone else to deal with rejection of one or two calls when it's not their company or personal reputation on the line.

"I always understood how powerful good PR could be but didn't know the nuts and bolts about how to go about it. The coaching I did with Paula was easy and simple to follow and really lead me through all the steps that I needed to take to start building a PR strategy and the steps that I needed to put in place to carry them out. The newsletter is a great example of something I developed during one of the online courses. It started with a handful of readers and now has a monthly readership of over 2000 people made up of journalists, buyers and people that I have met along my business journey to date."

T

TIP SHEETS

Tip sheets are short, snappy, advice-based emails, which are excellent for helping you build your profile and status as an expert. I started really using them a few years ago when one of my clients drew up her list of top 10 publications - which included the financial pages of the Sunday Times, Daily Mail etc. Unfortunately she announced that she found the thought of getting on the phone to these people just too overwhelming. Despite all my coaxing and coaching, she just wasn't ready. So, we launched monthly tip sheets on her target area and guess what, within a couple of months (yes, as quick as that) they were calling her! By getting valuable professional advice out regularly she had proven that she knew her area and could be approached for expert comments and advice.

Here are 5 things you should know about tip sheets.

1. They are great for people and businesses that need to raise their profile as an expert. Perhaps, though, they are not so great if you're selling a product, although it can be done.

2. It's the persistence that matters most. You need to prove that you are a reliable source of advice.

If they keep getting your tips and advice they will, over time, acknowledge you as an expert.

3. Unlike press releases, tip sheets don't really need to be chased up. This means that they are a great low-maintenance PR tool.

4. You can of course recycle your content and use tip sheets in your newsletter, on your blog etc.

5. Write six months worth of tip sheets in advance and all you have to do is send them out on a regular date, say the 2nd of the month.

TWITTER

It took me a while to catch onto Twitter (*www.twitter.com*) and it was media coach Alan Stevens again that convinced me it was worth a try. As Alan explained to me, the idea is that by sending an SMS, or visiting the Twitter website, you can send out an alert on what you are doing, or perhaps even thinking, right now. This goes out to your followers and the idea is to amass as many followers as possible. You can follow others too, although it's a good idea to aim for having more followers than people you follow.

As I write this there are currently a number of very Twitter-savvy people who have followers in the thousands.

Alan told me a great story of how Twitter has brought him work.

"I was between appointments and decided to have a coffee at Starbucks in The Strand and Twittered this.

Ten minutes later I see a man walking towards me. It's a past client who had lost touch. He had seen the Tweet, decided to come and say hello and offer me some work. I honestly don't think I would have got the business any other way. And all within a matter of half an hour. It's one of the few social networking tools I'd actually pay for."

Barack Obama brought Twitter into his Presidential campaign in 2008, and both Stephen Fry and Jonathon Ross are well-known UK public Tweeters. I was even intrigued to find that my own sister, who works for Greenpeace in Beijing, has to Tweet about Greenpeace as part of her day to day activities.

Wealth coach Nicola Cairncross of *www.themoneygym.com* is another Twitter fan.

Nicola Cairncross
www.themoneygym.com

"I first realised the value and power of Twitter when I read a blog posting by Rich Schefren. He was talking about being in the audience of South by South West (big conference in the USA). He was 'tweeting' via SMS to his Twitter followers, about what the speaker was saying on stage – the new ideas coming out of the conference were immediately being disseminated through the Twittersphere, and thus the Blogosphere, almost instantaneously. Amazing! And it's a free service which is even more amazing!

"From a community building, social networking and internet marketing point of view, it's very powerful. You can set up your Twitter account so that when you tweet (think of a tweet as a mini-blog posting or update) it fires onto your Facebook account, your Ecademy account, your MySpace account, your blog sidebar and many, many other places. So think of your Twitter account as the glue that holds all your other social networking sites and your mobile network together.

"It's made a huge difference for us! As well as being great fun and a brilliant way to keep up with growing trends, hot topics and on top of the news, Twitter has become the second biggest source of free traffic to *www.themoneygym.com* second only to the Google search engine. Some say Google will end up buying Twitter, as Twitter functions also as a brilliant human driven search engine – sort of like Wikipedia crossed with Google! So Twitter is the first real competition Google has had for search, for ages.

"From a marketing point of view, in six months, I've built up a following of over 1200 people just by tweeting on topics with the occasional fun stuff thrown in – it's like a single opt-in mailing list in a way. We gain more followers per day on Twitter than opt in to our double-opt in mailing list. It's another route to reach people essentially. When I tweet, many of my 'followers' pick up on my tweets and re-tweet them out to their followers. The viral effect of that can be amazing (if you want people to do this, keep your tweets to under 110 characters to enable them to put RT and your twitter name in – for example RT @wealthcoach which you can see takes up 15 of their 140 characters allowed).

"I really believe that social networking, of which Twitter is an essential part, is crucial for ANY business who want to use attraction marketing rather than push marketing. For a start it's so affordable – most of the elements being completely free.

"It's all about building a loyal fanbase of people who love your product, want to buy from you, but more importantly regard your company as a set of human beings, even friends, who are more than just a faceless corporate brand who don't care about them."

Nicola's experience is very like mine – just by posting regular alerts you'll find that your followers seem to grow organically. You just have to figure out what it is you are going to Tweet about.

Marketing guru Nikki Pilkington of *www.businessontwitter.co.uk* is another Twitter convert and has kindly let me use some of her tips on using Twitter for business.

TIP ONE: KEEP CUSTOMERS INFORMED

Using short bite-size messages, you can keep new and potential customers informed about forthcoming product updates. You can create business from Twitter by directing customers to your website through clickable links within the Twitter messages.

TIP TWO: LET CUSTOMERS SIGN UP

Customers can be offered the option of signing up to your Twitter campaign when they buy your product or services. This connects you with customers that are already actively interested in hearing more about what you have to offer; completely avoiding wasting your budget on the disinterested. Twitters actively choose to 'Follow' a flow of messages.

TIP THREE: IT'S IMMEDIATE

Twitter is immediate; it takes seconds to message thousands of customers. If you need to create buzz around product changes, your customers can be the first to find out about it.

TIP FOUR: MARKET RESEARCH

You can perform rapid market research by sending a question out to thousands of potential customers who can each respond instantly with a one-word answer.

TIP FIVE: DEVELOP A FOLLOWING

Develop a following. Existing customers like to know about products and services before everyone else. Build a loyal following by leaking them exclusive information.

You can follow Nikki on Twitter by going to *www.twitter.com/nikkipilkington*

U

USING A PR COMPANY
TAKING ON A FREELANCER

Generally, a freelancer will have more than one client and will probably either work from their own premises or home, or come onto your premises for a set number of days each week or month.

Although you can advertise for a freelancer via the Media Guardian, PR week and even agencies, I believe that the best way to get a great freelancer is through word of mouth and this means doing some local networking.

It's a good idea to start doing this long before you desperately need a freelancer as it can take a while the find the perfect person for you. However, asking other companies who use freelance PR help for their thoughts on their current PR (plus any tips they have on how to get the best out of them) is the safest way to make sure that you find someone who can deliver.

WHAT TO LOOK FOR IN A FREELANCER

It's a sensible idea to choose someone who has non-competing clients. If you're a shoe designer, hiring a PR who handles your arch-rival can cause obvious problems. If The Times phones up and wants a shoe designer (but only one) for their fashion spread, then who are they going to choose? Agencies often handle similar clients but this is slightly different as most agencies are large enough to have more than one person working on an account and often the rivalry and competition between the teams can work in your favour.

Find someone who has enough time for you. Do they have outside help themselves (some have Virtual Assistants to handle their admin)? How easy is it to arrange a meeting with them? If they can fit you in any day this week this might be a bit worrying as they might be a bit too quiet (i.e. they have no clients) but if you can't be seen for three weeks that doesn't bode too well for the future.

Someone reasonably local will help. Virtual working is all well and good but what happens when you want to set an emergency meeting? Knowing that your PR is at least within an hour or two makes sense. Alternatively, do make sure that they are au fait with conference calls.

Choose someone who is set up to work virtually. Do they have a mobile phone for all-round contact? A fax? Skype? Most freelancers do, but it makes sense to check.

Look for someone who has a fresh attitude. Yes, having a PR that specialises in hair salons is great if you are a hair salon. They are used to talking to the right magazines, have all the contacts you need and know the industry. But if someone doesn't come from the right background don't mindlessly disregard them. Having a fresh eye and a thirst for new angles and ideas might result in you getting more than just a revamped campaign that they did for a different hair salon two years ago.

And When You've Found Them…

WORKING FROM YOUR OFFICE

Give them the same respect and facilities as everyone else on your staff. Slotting them into the corner to work and only letting them have access to the computers when Dave is on his lunch break and doesn't need his machine is insulting (but it happens a lot) and you won't keep your freelancer for long.

WORKING VIRTUALLY

Stay in touch with them. It does neither of you any good to leave them to their own devices and just let them just get on with it. A friendly call to chat about how things are going at least every other day when you are in the middle of a project makes sense.

OTHER RULES

Pay them promptly as nothing annoys freelancers more than having to chase invoices.

CHOOSING AN AGENCY

Choosing an agency can be easy. You could be lucky and stumble across the right mix of people with the right attitude, creativity and dynamism that suits your business. But, then again, you might hunt around for months, looking for that elusive quality you deem so important.

My advice is to go with your gut instinct. Meet the people who would be responsible for your account, not just the head honcho who goes out and gets the accounts. Talk to your potential team and find out how creative and proactive they really are. How many other accounts would they be working on? Will there be one stable person that is going to oversee your account?

Asking an agency to pitch for your account is all well and good if you're MTV or a household name, but many agencies are now charging for their time to put a pitch together. Do be aware of this if you suddenly get asked "Would you like us to put a pitch together for you?" Always ask if there is a fee involved first.

HOW TO FIND A PR COMPANY

The trade journal PR week is a great resource. You can also check out the job ads put in by PR companies to see the sort of clients that they carry. But the short-cut would be to check out their website *www.prweek.co.uk* and use their directory service to locate PR companies by location or specialities.

Word of mouth is another popular way to find a company, and usually helps you pin-point those that fit in with your vision, and those that don't. Again, networking is the best way to do this and do feel free to ask probing questions such as "Are you happy with your PR agency?"

HOW TO NARROW THE FIELD

Choose an agency that specialises. If you are in the health sector it makes sense to choose an agency that knows the journalists from that area and can perhaps offer leverage with other clients (freebies, interviews etc) to get you some coverage.

Choose an agency that does its own PR. You should see them at the trade shows, in the industry press. They should have a presence.

Choose an agency that has clients roughly the same size as you. If all their other clients are bigger then you might easily get overlooked.

If you've already got links and a relationship with journalists or editors on the magazines and publications you want to target, don't be afraid to ask them for their advice. Who do they enjoy working with – and who do they find a bit too pushy or ineffective?

Paula Gardner

V

VIRTUAL ASSISTANTS

Virtual Assistants, or VAs, can be a tremendous help in a PR campaign. Although they aren't PR professionals and you can't expect them to have the contacts and knowledge of a PR freelancer, choose the right one and you'll find that they can contribute a great deal to your PR.

Firstly, there are VAs and there are VAs. (Oh, just in case you don't know a virtual assistant is an assistant who works virtually, usually on the admin side of the business). If you're looking for a VA who can help you on the PR side you'll first need to decide what you want them for.

Is it the admin that goes along side a PR campaign? Do you want them to put media lists together, research places for articles in the Internet and submit them for you? Most VAs will be able to handle this, and in my opinion, it's a good use of their time as these are boring, mind-numbing jobs that need to be delegated as soon as possible.

Or do you need a VA who can copywrite and put together a press release or email a journalist and hit the right mark? If so find out if they've done this sort of thing before and get them to write a trial release for you.

Or perhaps you're looking for someone who can take the most dreaded job of all off your hands – cold calling the press. This is the trickiest one – whilst it's very easy to assess someone's writing skills, with PR or sales skills it's different. You'll be looking for someone who is chatty, confident and with a bit of personality. Perhaps someone with a background in sales (although you'll need to explain that the PR approach is much less pushy).

Finally, although many people do use virtual assistants from anywhere in the country (I even know one well-known Irish marketer with an assistant in Australia), I personally like to have the option of being able to meet up, even if it's only once every few months. It works better for me as I like to get to know them and their approach, and think this time can be used for you to explain your big business goals and where you see them in your strategy, rather than just have them concentrating on one task after another.

VACATIONS

Clients often ask me whether they should bother sending out releases etc during the months of August and December as they are guessing that many of the press will be on holiday. My opinion is that this is the very best time as so many people presume the same thing and you have more of a chance of a journalist spotting you.

My advice is to keep the system running as normal. Once you let it slip it's very hard to get back on top of it again, and I speak from experience!

W

WHEN PR DOESN'T WORK

If your PR doesn't appear to be working, it's vital to look at why before you decide to give up. Yes, there are times when PR isn't the answer, but they are far and few between.

- Your first step is to ask yourself some questions and be prepared to answer honestly.

- Can you, hand on heart, say that you have given this your full attention and a decent amount of time each week?

- Do you feel that you have been approaching the right target market for you?

- And do you think that you have been approaching your target publication with spot-on stories that they should be interested in, or just cobbled something together and hoped that they'll go for it?

- Have you employed a number of different mediums (press releases, tip sheets, blog, twitter, articles etc) all reinforcing the same message for at least three months?

- Have you followed up your mail-outs with calls to the press to get feedback?

- If you have had coverage, did that coverage produce sales or newsletter sign-ups? If not, was that a result of the coverage being wrong (i.e. wrong market), or were people disappointed when they visited your shop or site and didn't follow through?

Whether you are a one-man band doing everything from making to delivering goods and planning and carrying out your own PR and marketing, or a large organisation employing specific PR people or an agency, re-evaluating your PR is something you should do on at least a quarterly basis.

So, how do you do this?

The easiest and most obvious step is to look at your new customers and clients over that past quarter and explore what brought them to you. Was it the article in the local newspaper, or the time you appeared on Radio Sunset and they just had to give you a call the next day? Or did they find you through a search engine or referral from a past customer?

Place your new business (in financial terms) against what you have spent on PR. Was it financially viable? If yes, then great. If not, hold on; don't give up just yet. Ask yourself is your PR an investment? Are you expecting to see the pay off this year, or will it take a few years to push you into the forefront of your market?

Does PR help you look credible enough to charge a certain price for your goods or services, or do you just get a kick out of being in the FT (and why not!)? There can be other rewards which come with PR, and being aware of what you are getting out of it can help with your plans for the next year.

So, what if it isn't working? Then you have some choices.

- Try harder and put more resources, more time and effort into it.

- Try another way. Perhaps the time has come when you do need the help of a professional. Or, alternatively, you may decide that you and your staff can do it as well as your current PR, for a fraction of the price.

- Try something else. You can experiment and for six months put your time, effort and resources into something else like marketing, direct mail or networking and see what percentage that return brings on your efforts.

If things aren't happening for you, don't sit back and hope. Be proactive, make decisions and take action!

WIN, WIN, WIN

Competitions have long been a great way to get press coverage for the fraction of the price you would pay for an advert. Of course, over the years the amount of gear publications want as a competition prize has gone up enormously. Where you could previously get away with offering 5 CDs, it's now more like a minimum request of 50.

The trick with competitions is to find out how much space you will be getting and whether there will be an accompanying photograph, which will help you gauge what it's worth to you. And, of course, you have to bring both the publication and where the competition will be placed, into the equation. A lovely two page spread with a write up is pretty much a no brainer, but if you're one box on a competition page along with many others then it's not quite so attractive.

If you're keen on the idea of competitions (and it's a great way of getting rid of old stock) then consider concentrating online, and making people click through to your site to find the answer to a question as part of the process. This way people at least visit your site and whilst many of them are just there for the prize, there will be a proportion of these who will genuinely be interested and hopefully sign up for your newsletter or further information.

X

EXCITEMENT

Okay, so I cheated here, but I deliberately wanted to emphasise how important it is that your excitement for your product or service shines through anything you send out. The main advantage a business owner or small company has in doing their own PR is that they are close to the passion that started the business in the first place. Whilst a PR agency or freelancer can (but not always) provide good contacts and experience, to them you will always be another job. What you have is your passion and that can be much, much more alluring. If you're feeling jaded it's not the time to put together the next release, much less make calls to journalists. You'll need to take some time out, whether that's half an hour at the coffee shop or a long walk with the dog, and refocus on what's brought you here in the first place. Some questions you might like to ask yourself are:

- What difference (to others) did you think you could make when starting this business?
- Can you remember that moment when you decided to go for it?
- What did it feel like?
- Has anything changed?

Another action which helps keep the excitement alive is to keep a file (computer or cardboard, or both) of clients' and customers' positive comments. You use these for testimonials, but just taking a look at these on a regular basis can lift your spirits and remind you why you are doing what you are doing.

Y

YOU

The key to successfully doing your own PR is you, and understanding yourself. When I meet clients for a consultation I not only make the effort to find out about their businesses and the background that brought them to me, but I also try to find out as much as possible about them. What do they enjoy doing (in a PR and marketing context)? Are they good writers, or more confident speaking? Do they enjoy meeting other people and making strategic alliances, or are they happier sat alone with a computer for company.

Over the years I have learnt that even though I might intuitively know that the best way for a certain business to get publicity might be xyz, if the person handling the PR isn't happy using those methods, then it just won't happen. It's far better to learn what makes them tick and sits well with their strengths, and work with that.

And that goes for you too. What do you enjoy doing? You're far more likely to concentrate on tasks that bring your enjoyment than slave away at something you hate. Think about your strengths and talents. Do they lie in writing, or public speaking perhaps? Or maybe you're a natural deal-maker? Thinking about you will design your

PR campaign uniquely around you, and make it much more likely to be something that you keep at long term.

If you're unsure get some feedback from friends and colleagues, either face to face, or set up an anonymous survey where they can answer without fear of offending you.

YOU TUBE

You Tube (*www.youtube.com*) is another example of how social media is playing an increasingly larger part in PR campaigns. It's not for everyone, and I feel it works really well when used for a youth market, but this might well change in the future. After all, even Barack Obama has his own channel on You Tube!

Other big players include Apple (of course) who use it to advertise the iPhone, and Coca Cola. One notoriously successful US campaign is for Blendtec, a home blender. Blendtec have come up with a series of short videos where they blend various household objects such as a TV remote, hearing aid, golf balls, an iPhone and even a Tom Tom satellite navigation system.

Checking today I see that the Blentec iPhone slot has had 2,676,353 views. How's that for brand promotion?

Over here wealth coaching company The Money Gym have used You Tube for testimonials, wealth coaching surgeries and introducing their various wealth coaches. It's a move that has kept them at the edge of technology and marketing. As wealth coaches who show people how to build businesses, it's something that helps them walk their talk.

And of course the beauty of You Tube is that it's the content that matters, not fancy editing, props and actors. It also brings a much more human face to the business, something which I feel has become more and more important recently. With a few creative ideas, a You Tube campaign could be a fantastic weapon in anyone's PR arsenal.

Paula Gardner

Z

ZEST

Zest is what I hope that I have left you with at the end of reading this book. My aim here has been to offer you a range of options and let you decide what to try. If you do try something and it doesn't work, then just remember, it's all the more likely that the next thing you try probably will. Different activities work for different people and different business. The only way to find out is try them.

But you'll need to give them some time – say three to six months, to really be able to assess if they are working for you. And, bring in one new activity at a time. Master and refine that before bringing in something else.

Remember, once those journalists start responding and the customers start buying, it can be a lot of fun!

I'm always happy to hear from readers, whether it's with their own story of what worked for them, or a question about PR as a result of reading this book. You can always email me at Paula@doyourownpr.com, or search my website *www.doyourownpr.com* for more ideas and articles on PR.

Paula Gardner

Extras

Whilst I can talk about press releases and tip sheets until I'm blue in the face, nothing quite beats actually seeing some for yourself. So, I've included some example of real life releases and tip sheets that have worked.

PRESS RELEASES

Here's a release that has what I call an internal hook – it's about the business itself.

Beyond France
A Slice Of Rustic Hungarian History

If you thought that France was the place to go for vintage linen then think again. Beyond France (www.beyondfrance.co.uk) brings you a range of rustic natural, embroidered and hand-dyed fabrics all originally homespun in rural Hungary between 1820 and 1940.

UK based mother of 3 Maud Lomberg spends 10 days a month travelling through Hungary on a mission to find vintage fabrics made by the village women who worked the flax from their own land. In those days, what wasn't put to work immediately was stockpiled for future use. And today, Beyond France has given those fabrics new life as items such as cushion and pillow covers, tablecloths, throws, bed sheets, mattress covers and tea towels.

Every last scrap of material is put to good use, with left-overs being made into goodies such as rag rugs and

---

lavender hearts – you can't get much more ecological than that! There are even cart covers which make great bed throws or over sized tablecloths, or, for the creative, hand embroidered grain or flour sacks which can be made into curtains or bench covers, or even an unusual laundry bag.

Beyond France came into being when, seven years ago, Maud (who was sourcing antiques) came across a Hungarian gypsy who had a gorgeous stack of quirky, home-spun natural linen. Now this sun bleached natural look is Beyond France's signature range. Later, Maud found two local traditional dyers (there used to be over 200!) who dye using custom made wells. This meant that Beyond French could now offer hand-dyed linen in stunning indigo, fresh petal pink, sumptuous Hedgerow Purple or soft Lavender Blue. Patterns such as Polka Dots and Roses are hand printed on to the linen using traditional printing blocks which have been in use for at least 100 years.

Every trip out to Hungary is an adventure – Maud never knows what she'll find, which means that what's available changes onsite regularly, and once gone, may never come up again – a real opportunity to bag something gorgeous and truly unique.

Originally created for every day use, Beyond France vintage linens are both unique and durable – a slice of everyday rustic Hungarian history.

For more information visit www.beyondfrance.co.uk or speak to _____ on _____

And here's one that has used the TV programme The Apprentice as its hook.

You're Fired - But They're Inspired

Practically everyone who watches The Apprentice sits there thinking that they could do better than the contestants.

Now, six young people from Hackney are proving they can do just that. As part of Cup of Clearworth management training challenge (www.acupofclearworth.co.uk) a group of young people from the Robert Levy Foundation* is given a taste of what it's like to plan and run their own business – a Piaggio coffee cart.

They're being taken through fundamental business skills, and making decisions such as name and logo (they chose a "A Cup of Youth"), branding and location, strategies for dealing with the competition, costs and price setting pricing (including mastering a spreadsheet), promotions, team goals and rules and customer service.

Sir Alan Sugar said in a recent interview with The Telegraph, "If we are to get Britain working again we have to teach children from a very early age to have a work ethic. When I was a child I desperately wanted to become self-sufficient, children don't have that desire now." The Coffee Cart Project is very in keeping with Sir Alan's thinking.

The young people - Tarjah, Christopher, Joe, Amira, Henni, TJ and Elliot – have to make their own decisions, live by their mistakes and celebrate their successes.

And, of course, one of their aims is to prove that six young people with no previous business experience can do better than the highly confident high-fliers from last year's Apprentice. After all, who can forget their coffee cart challenge where Andy bought over double the amount of milk they needed, Jadine called the boys back when they were in full sales flow, and Gerri picked a disastrous location outside the greasy spoons of Chapel Market where they didn't have a hope competing?

In contrast, The Cup of Clearworth Coffee Cart Project participants took £223 in sales on their first outing, of which they gave £60 to sports relief.

The programme, currently being run in conjunction with EDF, takes fast-track managers through business and coaching skills and they, in turn, coach and mentor the young people through planning and running their business. Even though they haven't yet completed the programme, participant Amira feels her future is now much more hopeful:

"I have learned so much and I'm getting up at four in the morning to make the most of this opportunity. I've had a glimpse of how I can use my brain and make money and I love it! Although the pressure is huge, I've learned that that's business, and the look on people's faces when I give them their coffee is worth it. I was planning to go back to an ordinary job in a hairdressers, but now I'm thinking seriously about what I can do with my future as I don't want to waste what I've learned here."

The 29th April sees the official launch at The Tate Modern of the EDF Senior Management Programme, which includes the Coffee Cart Project. Both Jim Knight, Minister of State for Schools and Learners, and Tim Campbell, the first winner of the first Apprentice, will be talking about the importance of education. They'll be joined by Lesley Everett, international image consultant and author of "Walking Tall", who has worked with everyone on this project.

Eager to reach as many schools and communities as possible, Clearworth believe that this is not only a fantastic training and socially responsible project for organisations, but a chance to really make a difference to the future of young people. And the more that get that chance, the better.

We'd love you to come along on the 29th and meet everyone, and especially the young people who are working so hard.

For more information on the Coffee Cart project please visit www.acupofclearworth.co.uk or speak to head barista Chloe Cox on 07768 742616. For Press enquiries contact Paula Gardner on 07941 244343 or email paula.gardner@clearworth.com

* 16 year-old Robert Levy was murdered a few yards from his home in Hackney, whilst trying to stop a fight. The foundation was set up in his name and aims to work with young people, supporting them in engaging in positive activities, training or employment.

TIP SHEETS

Here is an example of a series of tip sheets I put out in January 2008.

Tip Sheet No 1: Boost Your PR with your 2008 PR Resolutions from Do Your Own PR

This is naturally the time of year when we make plans for our businesses and their future. Paula Gardner from PR Training company Do Your Own PR has put together a short series of suggested resolutions to make the whole process much more painless and many times more effective.

Resolution No 1: Trim Off Some Fat

If you're going to make 2008 the year you do some serious PR and promotion, and the reason that you haven't actually done it up until now is that you've been too busy, you need to trim off some fat. And by fat I mean pointless wasting of time (my particular waste of time is Spider Solitaire). But sometimes wasting time can come in much more respectable packaging, like spending your time packing goods and carting them to the Post Office when you could easily pay someone to do that for you and devote the freed up time to PR. Or taking part in meetings and networking events that don't really bring in the results to justify the effort. Take a look at where you are wasting time and work out what you can cull to make way for time spent on PR.

Tip Sheet No 2: Boost Your PR with your 2008 PR Resolutions from Do Your Own PR

Resolution 2: Take Some Exercise

Just as one session a month at the gym isn't going to deliver results, one marathon PR session per month won't either. You need to devote regular and sustained effort and attention. But the great thing is that done persistently and consistently most forms of PR – blogging, articles, press releases, tip sheets etc – will deliver results.

Tip Sheet No 3: Boost Your PR with your 2008 PR Resolutions from Do Your Own PR

Resolution 3: Read more

You wouldn't believe how often I get people coming to me who want to get into the papers or magazines and yet look down their nose at actually picking one up and reading it. Forego getting your news fix from the Internet and start reading a daily newspaper. Not only will it will do your business and networking credibility no end of good to have all the latest news and gossip at your fingertips, but you'll get ideas for stories, news of surveys, ideas for articles all delivered to you in one neat package every day. Vary what you read and make it a mission to once a month buy something you really wouldn't usually consider, whether it's Vanity Fair or Accountancy Age. Pinch ideas, get inspired – the more you read the more you'll find yourself brimming over with creativity.

Tip Sheet No 4: Boost Your PR with your 2008 PR Resolutions from Do Your Own PR

Resolution 4: Stop Smoking

We don't want smoke, we need fire. Rediscover your passion, your reason for doing what you do in the first place and connect with that. Find out why your clients and customers choose you and use that as a driving force of your campaign. Half-heartedness just doesn't work.

Paula Gardner

Glossary

DPI – Dots per inch. A method of measuring low or high resolution on photographs. The more dots per inch, the sharper the reproduction will be, but also the harder it will be to send via email.

RSS - Really Simple Syndication. A method by where people can sign up to your blog and have updates sent direct to them, rather than having to visit your blog to get them

SEO – Search Engine Optimisation. The science or art of getting your website as high as possible within the search engine rankings. Many marketers believe that any site lower than the third page might well as not be on there.

VA – Virtual Assistant. A person who works virtually but helps out in your business, often on the administrative side.

About Paula Gardner

Paula was born and brought up in South Wales and went on to study English and American Literature at Kent University. Whilst she had spent her teens dreaming of hopping between the London and New York offices of Cosmopolitan magazine, she was brought down to earth when her best post-degree job offer came from The Local Government Chronicle.

Paula Gardner
www.doyourownpr.com

After six months of writing articles on various local council's approach to choosing litterbins, Paula decided that her skills might be put to better use in the more glamorous environment of music PR.

She spent the early 1990's working in the music industry on clients such as George Michael, Bananrama and Sinitta. Day to day jobs ranged from co-ordinating large-scale press events to running out to get sandwiches for "celebrities". After two years she left to set up her own PR company, Paula Gardner PR, based at London's St Katherine's Dock. Specialising in PR for the restaurant and entertainment industry, Paula worked with high profile clients such as Red, L'Escargot and Soho's O bar, before deciding to move from doing PR, to teaching it.

In 2002 Do Your Own PR was created, along with the 30 day Do Your Own PR course. And since then Paula has helped hundreds of small businesses learn the skills necessary to raise their company or personal profile.

Paula's first book, Get Noticed: How to Boost your Small Business Profile in 30 days or less, was published in 2005, and since then she has written on the subject of PR and marketing for numerous publications including The Sharp Edge, Fashion Capital, The Stage and Play and Party Magazine.

Paula has spoken about the power and how-to of PR at various conferences, including the Everywoman conference, Women In Film and TV, CIDA, and Allen Carr Easy Way To Stop Smoking Now.

Paula still writes for a number of consumer magazines and websites around the subjects of health and lifestyle. She is also the founder and editor of women's book website *www.chicklit.co.uk* which was included in The Times Top Ten Havens for Busy Women.

Do Your Own PR offers a range of PR courses to help you learn about running a PR campaign for your business. Written by Paula Gardner, the author of the small business PR guide Get Noticed, available from Amazon, these courses cover Do Your Own PR, Building A Cult newsletter, How To Write A Press Release, Writing Copy to Sell and Double Your Clients Through Networking and more.

For more details please visit:

www.doyourownpr.com/products.asp

GET
NOTICED

HOW TO BOOST YOUR
SMALL BUSINESS PROFILE
IN 30 DAYS OR LESS
PAULA GARDNER

www.bookshaker.com

MEDIA
Masters

Insider Secrets from the
big names of broadcast,
print and social media

**Alan Stevens &
Jeremy Nicholas**

www.bookshaker.com